The comple

Distributed by:

UK
A.A. Publishing
(A Division of the
Automobile Association)
Fanum House
Basingstoke
Hampshire RG21 2EA

Australia
Gordon & Gotch Ltd,
25-37 Huntingdale Road,
Burwood
Victoria 3125

First published and produced
in Australia in 1990 by:

T.P. Books & Print Pty Ltd
Suite 13, 3 Moore Lane
Harbord Village
Harbord NSW 2096

In Association with:

Tourist Publications
6 Piliou Street
Koliatsou Square
112 55 Athens, Greece

© Copyright Tourist Publications 1990

Editorial Directors:	L. Starr,
	Y. Skordilis
Authors:	Kerry & Geoff Kenihan
Typography:	M. Roetman
Design:	C. Mills
Layout:	C. Mills
Photo-setting:	Deblaere Typesetting Pty Ltd
Photographs:	Kerry Kenihan
	Government of India Tourist Office
	Howard R. Houck
Maps:	Judy Trim

Printed in Australia

ISBN 1-872163-25-4

All rights reserved. No part of this book may be reproduced or transmitted in any form or by any means, electronic or mechanical, including photocopying, recording or by an information storage and retrieval system, without written permission from the publisher.

Due to the wealth of information available, it has been necessary to be selective. Sufficient detail is given to allow the visitor to make choices depending on personal taste, and the information has been carefully checked. However, errors creep in and changes will occur. We hope you will forgive the errors and omissions and find this book a helpful companion.

ABOUT THIS GUIDE

Bombay, Gateway to India, is the New York of the East, one of the world's most populous cities and as cosmopolitan as any sophisticated visitor could desire.

This guide introduces you to the metropolis which is the centre of the largest movie-making industry on earth to be entertained, to eat more lavishly and variedly than ever before and to discover Asia's largest seaport.

Part I traces the history of India and Bombay, once a tiny fishing village, and informs on the nation's culture, religions, language, government, flora, fauna, geology, climate etc.

Part II will take the visitor step by step through the streets of the city past all its historic and new attractions then on a relaxing excursion to golden Goa with its glorious, tropical beaches, hilled villages and a fascinating heritage from Portugal. Then comes a short sojourn at Aurangabad with its amazing, nearby cave temples.

Part III is a full list of accommodations with practical tips.

More practical advice on travelling in Bombay and India generally is given in **Part IV**, including food and shopping and how to seek help if required.

Business travellers will find their special **Part V** of assistance. Colour maps are included.

Bombay is an ideal place to begin a first visit to India but it is also a city to which the seasoned traveller feels compelled to return. Enjoy its bustle and beauty.

Acknowledgements

We are indebted to the **personnel** of the **Government of India Tourist Office, Sydney**, also **Bombay** and **Goa**, for their support and interest, **Air India** for international transport to and from India and to **Australian Airlines** for authors' connecting flights in their home country.

Table of Contents

PART I - INDIA AND HER PEOPLE

A Quest for Discovery 9
Geology and Geography 11
Climate 11
Flora and Fauna 12
Government 14
Education 16
Commerce and Industry 16
Religions 18
    Hinduism 18
    Buddhism 19
    Jainism 20
    Sikhism 20
    Zoroastrianism 20
    Judaism 21
    Christianity 22
    Islam 24
The Peoples of India 24
Meeting People 25
Indian Languages 28
History and Culture 30
Indian Glorious Architecture 40

PART II - BOMBAY, GATEWAY OF INDIA   47

Discovery Fort Bombay
and the South Gateway of India 48

  The Elephanta Caves 50
  The Prince of Wales Museum 53
  Jehangir Art Gallery 54
  Bombay University and Rajabai Clock Tower 54
  Flora Fountain 56
  Horniman Circle 57
  Victoria Railway Terminus 57
  Bombay Municipal Corporation 58
  Nariman Point 60
  Afghan Church 61
  World Trade Centre 63
  CENTRAL BOMBAY 63
  Temples and Traffic 63
  Taraporewala Aquarium 63
  Chowpatty Beach 64

Malabar Hill	65
Jain Temple	66
Hanging Gardens	67
Mani Bhavan	69
Mahalaxmi Temple	70
Haji Ali's Mosque and Tomb	70
Mahalaxmi Racecourse	70
Nehru Planetarium	71
Worli Dairy	72
Victoria Gardens and the Zoo	72
Victoria and Albert Museum	72
Marvelous Markets	73
Fabulous Films	75
OUT FOR THE DAY	76
Panthers, Lions and Caves	76
The Beaches of Bombay	78
GO GO GO TO GOA	79
Goa Dourada - Golden Goa	82
SOUTH GOA	88
Churches, Temples and Beaches	88
Trains and Waterfalls	91
Niceties of the North	93
CAVING IN TO INDIA	96
Ellora and Ajanta	96
Daulatabad Forol	97
Ellora Caves	98

PART III - ACCOMMODATION

Hotels	105
Bombay	106
Goa	112

PART IV - PRACTICAL INFORMATION

A-Z Summary	116

PART V - BUSINESS GUIDE 185

MAPS

Bombay	100
India	195

INDEX 196

PART I
General Introduction

Typical central India gentleman

INDIA AND HER PEOPLE

A QUEST FOR DISCOVERY

'All my life I have been engaged in a quest - the discovery of my own country - India. During this life's journey of discovery, I have found much of my country that inspired me, much that interested me and much that made me understand a little of what India was and is today. And yet India, with the weight of ages behind her and with her urges and desires in the present, has only been partially discovered by me and I am continually finding out new faces of her many-sided personality that continually surprise me ...'

Jawaharlal Nehru

If former Prime Minister, Jawaharlal Nehru, the architect of modern India and one of its greatest visionaries, spent a lifetime in scratching the surface for the soul of his country, it is unlikely that the visitor will penetrate more deeply into a land that will not fail to awe, stimulate and enthral. But even a relatively short experience of the kalaidescope of India's culture, embracing its civilization, architecture, music, dance, painting and sculpture, fairs and festivals, traditional crafts and its tempting cuisines, will weave a spell that will never be broken. India's scenery is as diverse as it is dramatic, from the towering, snow-capped Himalayas descending into desert, rolling plains, tropical forests and beaches washed by three seas.

Its wildlife will stir the imagination of anyone who has ever read the stories of Bombay-born English author and poet, Rudyard Kipling, or any, who as a child, was captivated by pictures of panthers, tigers, elephants and monkeys. India is unlike many other countries which have been totally modernized in the 20th century. While its great cities such as Bombay offer sophistication, deluxe facilities and the high life to those who seek it, there are also smaller cities, towns and villages which have stood still in time. Therefore in India the visitor is presented with rare opportunity - to step into a mystic, living past.

International tourism has come late to India. It is to the traveller's advantage that this vast sub-continent below Asia is blooming in an era of world tourism. India has not made the mistake of some other nations where great monuments to past glories have been torn down to make way for modern developments or even relocated far away from their original sites. India's past still lives as vibrantly as its diverse peoples with their many and varied religions

India and Her People

and the tourist industry is serving to maintain the nation's heritage. In practical terms, one can live the past - in a former Maharajah's palace, a Hill Station resort or a luxurious houseboat, any of which are living echoes of the great and glorious British Raj.

One can also travel through seven cities on a royal vintage train of opulent carriages originally created for the princely rulers and British viceroys more than 80 years ago. Luxury modern hotels and beach resorts are the equal to the world's best. This surprises some new visitors who read of India being a third world country.

Away from the exotic, India provides exciting opportunities for adventure and sport, from skiing, mountain climbing, white water river rafting to hang gliding or joining a camel safari. Yet, in addition, the traveller in India will also meet the people who still hold sacred their life-giving rivers, worship the aimless cow and devoutly believe that their sins will be absolved when they wash their bodies in the holy River Ganges. The people regard their India as a cohesive whole yet the foreigner invariably experiences it as a series of fascinating places which developed in different centuries under several faiths and races. India's cosmopolitanism, its industry and the plight of its poor are easy to see. But its complexities and its paradoxes of old and new, rich and poor all blend to weave a tapestry that is an enigma. The temptation to understand is irresistable to the traveller.

Preparing for Festival

India and Her People

GEOLOGY AND GEOGRAPHY

Geologically, India is divided into three parts, the Himalayas, the Indo-Gangetic Plain and the Deccan Peninsula.

The great Himalayas in the north were once covered by sea, and were formed by layer upon layer of marine deposits. The 1,500- mile long mountain chain has roughly five longtitudinal divisions and it is separated from the Tibetan Plateau by the valleys of the Upper Indus and Brahmaputra rivers. Created in the Tertiary Age, there are more than 60 peaks rising above 24,000 feet, culminating in the world's highest mountain - Everest which is in Nepal and Tibet. The lesser Himalayas are a number of ranges reaching heights of 12,000 feet, enclosing valleys such as the Vale of Kashmir.

The Indo-Gangetic Plain is the geological depression between the folding of the Himalayas and the peninsula structure of India. In the eastern sections of the plain, deposits are chiefly alluvial while in the west, windblown material is significant. It consists of sands and muds. Nearly 25 per cent of India is drained by the River Ganges, known as the Mother of India.

The geological history of the Deccan Peninsula of India is extremely complicated. Its rivers are shorter and drain far less areas than the three great systems of the north -the Ganges, the Indus and the Brahmaputra.

Roughly triangularly shaped, India is the world's seventh largest country and is bordered by Pakistan in the north east, China to the north west and east, Nepal, Tibet, Bhutan and Bangladesh and Burma to the east. India's most southerly point, Cape Comorin, is on the eighth degree of latitude and the nation's most northerly frontier lies on the 37th. India has a land area slightly in excess of 1,260,000 square miles. Its coastline is washed by the Arabian Sea in the west and the Bay of Bengal in the east. The Indian Ocean lies to the south. The nation is divided close to its southern tip from the independent island of Sri Lanka just 30 miles across the Palk Straits at the nearest point.

CLIMATE

There are three main seasons in India - summer, winter and the time of the monsoon. The weather is generally pleasant throughout the winter months between November and March although in the northern plains, night

India and Her People

temperatures can be quite cold and, in the mountains, drop below freezing point. In Kashmir and the Himalayas, it is extremely cold under snow. Winter time in the south is warm without any real cold being experienced. The summer months between April and June are hot throughout India with the exception of the Himalayan foothills which are balmy by day and a little crisp at night. When temperatures soar, particularly in the south, the British-created hill stations provide cool retreats as does Kashmir.

Summer is followed by the breaking of the south west monsoon along the west coast and the rains extend gradually across the country. Apart from the south east parts of India, the greatest part of the annual rainfall is received between the end of June to the end of September. The south east area is influenced by the north east monsoon when annual rainfall is mostly experienced between mid-October and the end of December.

FLORA AND FAUNA

While the sub-continent of India has no flora naturally unique to its area, it boasts a huge diversity of trees, shrubs and flowers ranging from the southern tropical zones to the mid- temperate areas of the north. The country can be divided into three main botanical sections -Himalayan, western and eastern.

The Himalayan region abounds with conifers, poplar, plane and oak trees with colourful rhododendrons and magnolias among many other flowers. Tree growth is relatively rare and stunted in the Indus and Gangetic Plain regions although the deltas of both the Indus and the Ganges have dense, evergreen forests of trees and shrubs in which the mangrove is predominant.

There is also the spreading, significant banyun tree under which Lord Buddha preached his first sermon. Since, it has always represented reflection and spirituality. Thick forests still remain in the hilly sections of the south. Along the south east coast, particularly Goa where bougainvillea is brilliant in its variety of colours and profusion, there is tropical growth galore. India's main cultivated plants include rice, wheat, tea, coffee, fruit trees and, in the south, the coconut palm.

The deepest of links has always existed between the races of India and their natural environment. Perhaps nowhere is this more deeply rooted than in the relationship between man and the wildlife's vast plains and forests. This union with nature originates in antiquity when the holymen, who claimed perception of a world beyond

India and Her People

normal human experience, made ecstatic journeys on the backs of tigers. Animals were the vehicles on which the gods of India moved - the swan, the peacock, the snake, the bull, the monkey and the elephant, to name a few.

Today India is in the forefront of the nations of the world in preserving its natural heritage of fauna. India sees its wildlife as a natural treasure and the country abounds with wildlife reserves sheltering and preserving more than 500 species of mammals and countless birds and reptiles.

The Western Himalayas are the last refuge of the Kashmir stag, a sub-species of the red deer and they also harbour a diversity of natural fauna including the snow leopard, the black and brown bear, the Ibex, a type of wild goat, and the musk deer.

The forest area of the Himalayan foothills is one of the main habitats of the tiger. There are also leopards, elephants and deer.

These can be seen in the **Corbett National Park** which is threaded by the **Ramganga river**. Here, there are two types of crocodile. Monkeys also inhabit the north.

In the arid **State of Rajasthan** is the Ghana waterbird sanctuary at Bharatpur which has several hundred species of resident and migratory visitors. In Rajasthan can also be found (mainly in national parks,) rugged species of deer, tigers and in India's only desert, the **Barmer- Jaisalmer**, are desert wolf, cat and fox.

Winter sports

India and Her People

The central western State of Gujarat is refuge to the Asiatic lion, leopards and antelopes. It has cranes and flamingoes on its **Lake Nalsarovar** and the adjoining central State of Madhya Prudesh is the heart of tiger country in the nation's core. The **Kanha National Park** has also wild dog, deer and the area is known as Kipling Country because the famous Jungle Books were set here.

Elephant, gaur, wild dog, mouse deer, sloth bears and, occasionally, giant squirrels can be found in the south, particularly at Karnatal's Bandipur Tiger Reserve and Nagarhole. Kaziranga National Park, on the Brahmaputra's banks in Assam in the east, is home to the one-horned rhinoceros and the Indian wild buffalo. In Assam's thick, evergreen forests are leopards.

Cat bears and red pandas live in the eastern Himalaya's temperate forests. India also has wolves and panthers which may be seen by the visitor who has travelled the few kilometres from Bombay to Sanjay Gandhi National Park and the Kanheri Caves. Here, they roam but mostly at night.

Birds in India include parrots, four types of vulture, hawks, falcons, kingfishers, kites, herons, mynah birds and game birds are snipe, pigeons, partridges, quail and red jungle fowl.

In rural areas, snakes intrude into gardens and sometimes dwellings, mostly in the rainy season. There is the Russelian snake and also cobra which you'll see being charmed in the streets of Bombay, Delhi and some other cities. The Russelian snake has a lethal bite as does the small krait. Fish include trout, kingfish (excellent eating in Goa, in particular,) and carp. There are also crayfish, oysters, mussels and prawns. The cow, of course, is sacred. Dogs roam as strays or are kept as pets and a few cats can be seen around bazaars and markets where they keep the mouse population down. There are also water buffalo, sheep and goats.

GOVERNMENT

India is a Federal Republic firmly based on the inheritance of the British Westminster system of parliamentary democracy but with some relatively recent changes that are similar to the government of the United States.

There is a balance of administration and power between the central government in the Federal Capital of Delhi and 25 State governments. There are also seven territories in India which are administered by the central government.

India and Her People

Bombay skyline

This system was seen by the architects of independent India as the best way of serving the interests of the people and has been enshrined in the nation's Constitution.

The central government has two parliamentary houses, the lower house being the **Lok Sabha** or House of the People and an upper chamber called **Rajya Sabha** or the Council of States. There is universal adult franchise in India and the people elect nearly 500 members to the Lok Sabha while the Council of States has about 250 representatives. Both houses of parliament, together with the State Parliaments, are involved in electing the president of the nation but the office of president is more symbolic as a head of State with true power vested in the Prime Minister.

Since 1952, elections for the House of the People have been held approximately every five years and the majority party is invited by the president of India to form a national government and elect a Prime Minister.

Elections in India, both Federal and State are very colourful and frantic affairs with posters and party flags hung everywhere from the largest cities to the smallest villages. For the fortunate visitor at the time of an election, all of India seems to take on an atmosphere of passionate festival as Indians from all walks of life and religions enjoy the process of deciding who will govern them and how.

EDUCATION

While in theory, all Indian children have the right to free elementary education, in practice, the nation is still struggling to keep its children in school in a basically agrarian society of small holdings where the demands of manual labour still draw heavily on youth.

Yet primary schools can be found in even the smallest villages throughout India where dedicated teachers make do with facilities that would be considered totally inadequate by western standards. Most larger towns have secondary education and the great cities of India boast universities with very high standards that have enabled their graduates to find professional employment not only in India but in many other highly developed western countries. Increasing the literacy rate remains a constant target of the government - for public education on stemming the birth rate in a country of 800 million to be effective. While religious traditions, the desire for male progeny and a widely-held belief that many children will bring security to aged parents contribute to the population control problem, it is also apparent that increased literacy/education in adults can have an effect on the attitude of populate or perish.

COMMERCE AND INDUSTRY

With the departure of the British Raj, the leaders of newly- independent India had a grand design for the rapid industrialization of their country which, similarly to the People's Republic of China, was seen to depend on heavy industry and engineering. But, more than 40 years after independence, more than two thirds of the working population are still engaged in agriculture with much of this being inefficiently performed on small farms.

India's exports are still based mainly on textiles, Bombay having the largest textile industry. Specialized produce such as tea is an export money-earner but India has not been as successful as many third-world nations in creating successful light industry exports. Greater emphasis is now being placed on developing hi-tech industry with computers and other electronic goods in the forefront but India is still paying the price of protecting post-independence industries from foreign exports which resulted in minimizing the country's relatively cheap labour opportunities to develop industrially-based exports to the same

India and Her People

Children fishing before sunset

extent as other Asian nations such as Taiwan, South Korea, Malaysia and Singapore.

There are some exceptions to this rule which has seen the possibility of a large automotive industry inhibited by protectionist policies. For instance, the Indian film making industry is the world's largest. Food production in India has been steadily increasing and, in the last two decades of the 20th century, the nation has achieved a food surplus and is steadily improving agricultural methods and the use of modern fertilizers should see India emerge as a significant exporter of agricultural products in the future.

India's main stock exchange is in Delhi. Most major industry is centred on the cities of Bombay and Calcutta with most heavy industry in or around the latter city.

RELIGIONS

Because India practises more religions than any other nation on earth, this section is longer than you will read in most of our other travel guides. The majority of Indians are adherents to the Hindu faith, almost 85 per cent. The second largest group is Muslim. In decreasing order come Christians, Sikhs, Buddhists and Jains. Judaism and Zoroastrianism (one of the world's oldest religions and practised by the Parsis of which Bombay has most,) are also represented.

The oldest religion of all is Animism which is still professed by small groups of primitive tribespeople scattered in the southern mountain regions of the sub-continent.

Hinduism

Hinduism, which probably sprang from primitive Animism, has often been described by philosophers as more than a mere religion because of the unique lifestyle of its followers, coupled with an outlook of free thinking that does not prevent even an atheist from being a Hindu. In this sense, Hinduism is a way of life. The religion is not based on any single book of prophesy nor the revelation of any single teacher but on what Hindus see as Eternal Truth.

Unlike other great religions, Hinduism has few do and don't dogmas. It allows Hindus the freedom of their own individual search for spiritual experience and is extremely tolerant of all other faiths in the belief that the goal is the same. Hinduism recognises one god which, in the highest form, is **Brahma**, the universal soul or spirit transcending time and space but who has physical representations in the form of Brahma, the creator, **Vishnu**, the preserver and **Shiva**, the destroyer and, paradoxically, also the rejuvenator.

There is a female counterpart to each of this trinity. Brahma's consort is **Saraswati** while Vishnu's companion is **Lakshmi** and Shiva's 'other half' is **Shakti**, worshipped as the mother of the world and symbolizing the power by which the one god creates then destroys the world only to recreate it again. One of the interesting facets of Hinduism that it absorbed many of the gods and rituals of successive conquerors of India from primitive times. These gods were all accepted by Hinduism in the belief that they represented the one great god whom other peoples knew by different names. The result in modern day Hinduism is

India and Her People

a profusion of minor gods and goddesses   A basic tenent of the religion, which has been absorbed by other religions in turn, is the belief in reincarnation. Hindus believe that their soul continues through cycles of birth, death and rebirth until that soul becomes one with Brahma, never to be reborn again. The law of **Karma** or 'action' is also a corner-stone of Hinduism. Basically, Karma embodies the law of cause and effect and is not unlike the Judaic belief that, as one sows, so one shall reap. A Hindu's thoughts, deeds and words in this life will determine the nature of reincarnation.

Hinduism also offers its devotees three paths to attain union with Brahma. Most Hindus choose the simplest through devotion and worship of a form of god, observing strictly their prayers, rituals and festivals. A second way to reach the one god is through action in the form of **Karma Yoga** where both men and women seek their goal through selfless service in their daily work. The final and most difficult pathway chosen by very few is that of **Jnana Yoga**, the way of knowledge and wisdom.

The Hindu scriptures direct that rituals and pilgrimmages to holy places are the first step in the pathway to the one god. A second way is in the worship of the one god through statues and images and the highest form is through mental worship and meditation.

The mystical syllable 'Om' is the symbol of Brahma.

Buddhism

Although this religion was born in India, it rapidly spread to neighbouring Asian countries, particularly China, so that now every fourth human being is a follower of Buddha. The religion's founder was born a prince in the 6th century BC. Prince **Siddhartha** was deeply moved by sickness, poverty and death that he saw beyond his palace walls and, at the age of 29, he left his royal life to seek the knowledge of teachers before embarking on a life of asceticism.

After nearly six years of meditation, he reached a state of enlightenment and commenced 45 years of preaching. He became **Gautama** or the **Buddha** and he taught his followers four truths to end human suffering. Buddha's followers also believe in the law of Karma and reincarnation although the Buddha himself never taught the concept of a one god or the individual soul. Some of the Buddha's teachings have been absorbed into Hinduism and Buddha became one of the Hindu pantheon as the ninth incarnation of Vishnu, the preserver.

Buddhists must not injure any living thing. They must not steal, live in an unchaste manner, lie, steal nor consume alcohol or drugs. While there are relatively few Buddhists in India today, the religion was spread by monks throughout central Asia, China and Japan, beginning under the rule of the great emperor **Ashoka** in the third century BC.

Jainism

Like Buddhism, Jainism arose as a reaction to the personal excesses of early Hindu priests but it has never created a following of any significance outside of India. Like Buddha, the founder of Jainism, **Vardhamana Mahavira** was born in the 6th century BC and renounced life as the son of a tribal chief to spend the next 12 years in a life of penance before reaching a state of the highest knowledge. He spent his remaining 30 years in spreading his doctrine of rejecting material possessions and not injuring any other creature.

Like Buddhism, Jainism does not embrace a creative god. But it holds the concept of a personal soul going through cycles of death and reincarnation to break the earthly bonds of Karma. Jainism has a strong following in India today and its adherents base their lives on simplicity of living, charity, humility and forgiveness of others.

Sikhism

The most recent of all of India's great religions, Sikhism emerged in the 15th century AD through its founder, the **Guru Nanak**, during a time of invasions and suffering in the **Punjab** region. Nanak's teachings were greatly influenced by **Kabir**, a saint recognised by both Hindus and Muslims. The essence of the Sikh religion as revealed by the Guru Nanak is the fatherhood of one god and the brotherhood of man. Sikhism also recognises that all religions are seeking to teach the same truths.

Because of this, devotees of all religions can follow the Sikh way of service to both man and god. The Sikh religion emphasizes the work ethic, family life, communal obligations and moral values. Personal prayer and meditation is the way by which the Sikh reaches towards god. While Sikhs also believe in reincarnation, the religion is essentially a bridge between Hinduism and Islam.

Zoroastrianism

Originally the main religion of Persia, Zoroastrianism was brought to India in the 7th century AD when many of its followers fled as Arab conquerors converted their country to Islam. In India, they became known as **Parsis**, a name stemming from the region of Pars in Persia from which the majority of religious refugees came. Today, India has the largest number of Zoroastrianists in the world.

The religion was founded by **Zarathusthra** who was also called **Zoroaster** and it recognizes one supreme god, **Ahura Mazda**, the wise creator. The Supreme Lord has the sun as his emblem while on earth he is symbolized by fire - which is why a fire is kept constantly burning in all Parsi temples.

Zoroaster taught of a constant conflict between good and evil spirits in the world with man having to choose a path between goodness and evil. The religion directs its followers towards a life of hard work, communal service and charity and it is very tolerant towards all other faiths. Because of this, a present day Parsi is free to visit the temples and churches of all other religions and, in India, they often do.

Many Parsis moved from Gujarat to Bombay on the arrival of the British. Here, they contributed to the development of the port of Bombay and established many industries. Because of their hard work ethic, they aid the prosperity of any city in which they live and are also philanthropic in nature. Many buildings in Bombay, service and cultural organizations have been established because of Parsi benevolence.

Because the Parsis worship the sanctity and purity of the elements fire, water, earth and air, they will neither bury nor cremate their dead. The body of a Parsi is left in a Tower of Silence where the corps is soon consumed by vultures.

Judaism

The coming of Jews to India traditionally dates from the first destruction of the Temple in Jerusalem in the 6th century BC. These Jews who had fled Palestine were believed to have been ship-wrecked close to present day Bombay and their descendents are known in India as **Black Jews**.

The second wave of Jews reached India in the first century BC following the destruction of the second Temple in Jerusalem by the Romans. Both groups fled to Cochin after persecution by Arabs in the 16th century. A third wave arrived in the 19th century and these settled in the main cities. Today there are only about 5,000 followers of Judaism in India and, in recent years, many of India's Jews have migrated to Israel and western countries. Those remaining enjoy a life free of any form of anti semitism.

India and Her People

Christianity

Christ's apostle, **St. Thomas** was believed to have come to India in about 54 AD before Christianity reached Europe. The early Syrian Christians built a Church to St. Thomas in Kerala on the Malabar Coast close to the present-day city of Trivandram. St. Thomas is said to have crossed southern India and settled in a village near the modern city of Madras where he spent many years seeking to teach the words of Jesus Christ before being killed by a group who resented his evangelism.

Today's visitors to Madras can see a small cave on a low hill close to the Madras airport in which, tradition holds, the early Christian martyr lived. There is a second legend in India that points to **St. Bartholemew** being the first Christian missionary to visit and, even before the Renaissance, historians of the Middle Ages made references to Christian settlements in India. Legend and tradition changed to history with the arrival of **St. Francis Xavier** in western India in 1542 following the Portugese conquest of Goa. St Francis Xavier, whose casket is in the Church of the Born Jesus in Old Goa, draws Catholic pilgrims in their thousands to Goa each year.

The saint was followed by a wave of Portugese missionaries who travelled widely in India, some of them

Inside a temple

India and Her People

reaching the court of the Moghul emperor **Akbar the Great** and unsuccessfully attempting to convert him to Christianity.

After the Portugese, Catholic missionaries from other parts of Europe entered India and these were followed in the 18th century by protestant missionaries, particularly from Germany, Denmark and Holland. But the key to the spread of modern Christianity was the arrival of the British and their conquest of India resulted in an ascendency of the Anglican denomination above those which had come before.

Through two centuries of the British Raj, foreign missionaries spread throughout India and were particularly active in the more primitive tribal regions. India's Christians have contributed vastly to social welfare and education as well as providing medical and nursing support to the poor. The contribution of the Christian faith to modern Indian society is far greater than could be expected from the relatively small proportion of India's 800 million people who follow the way of Jesus Christ. This evangelical zeal and selfless humanitarianism was exemplified by such people as Mother Teresa. The father of independent India, Mahatma Gandhi, although not a Christian, was deeply influenced by its teachings and many of his most famous speeches and writings are punctuated with quotations from the New Testament.

India and Her People

Islam

Arab traders were the first to bring the teachings of the prophet **Mohammed** to India in the 7th century and they were followed by successive invasions by Muslims until the beginning of the 13th century. This saw the establishment of the first Muslim overlordship in Delhi. Muslim power extended from this base until only the most southern part of India was independent of Muslim India.

The great Moghul Empire was created in 1506 by **Barbur**. The greatest of his successors was **Akbar** who ruled from 1556 to 1605 and whose policy of religious tolerance brought a more-or-less lasting peace between Hindus and Muslims. Akbar's vision was continued by two others - Kabir and Nanak and Nanak the Guru who founded the Sikh religion with the goal of increasing mutual tolerance between Hindus and Muslims.

Islam's spirit of brotherhood has played a part in loosening the Indian caste system. The teachings of the prophet embodied in the Holy Koran are not far removed from those of the Old Testament of the Christian Bible. Islam recognizes only one god - Allah. The relative simplicity of Islam was a force in influencing Hindus to question the value of many of their traditional rituals yet, in India, the interaction of these two great faiths has resulted in aesthetic expression through poetry, music, art and architecture.

THE PEOPLES OF INDIA

Modern ethnologists agree that in the mists of pre-history, the Indian sub-continent was sparsely populated by a race of Negroid people possessing a primitive culture and probably related to aboriginal tribes still to be found in parts of Sri Lanka and the Indonesian island of Sumatra. It is still debated whether this race was ethnically linked with the Australoid tribes of Australia.

While still in an era of pre-history, India was invaded by other races from western Asia that have loosely been called **Dravidians**. These people slowly penetrated to the far south to be followed by a smaller infiltration of Mongol races from central Asia which entered the country from the north east. The blending of these two invading peoples with the original Aborigines is thought to have been completed when wave after wave of Aryan people swept into India through the mountain passes in the north-west. The Aryan invaders in turn were mostly absorbed and this has resulted in seven distinct racial types to be found in

India and Her People

modern India. Examples of the original Aboriginal race can still be identified with primitive tribal people of the jungles and mountains of southern and central India.

The Dravidian race can be distinctly identified throughout the south as far north as the Valley of the Ganges. A blending of Indo-Aryan races is more or less distinct to the regions of Rajasthan and the Punjab. The great majority of modern Hindus are a mixture of Aryan and Dravidian stock emanating from the Gangetic Valley but extending westward with a further blending of Indo-Aryan people has occurred.

Another distinct sub-race is the **Scytho-Dravidian** type found east of the Indus River. In Assam and the foothills of the eastern Himalayas, the people are of distinct **Mongul** inheritance, quite clearly related to the present population of China and Tibet. India's seventh distinct racial type are **Mongolo-Dravidians** who also appear to possess elements of Indo-Aryan blood and these people are represented principally in west Bengal. The English, of course, made their impact too, along with the Portugese to an earlier, lesser extent. There are pockets of Anglo-Indians in various parts, noteably Goa where the visitor will also meet Indians who could have been born in modern Lisbon.

It is hard to recognize all origins when you are visiting on a holiday. But the Sikh men are discernable for their colourful turbans beneath which all hair, never cut, is neatly wound. The dab of cosmetic colour worn by many Indian women on the forehead above the nose (and sometimes be-jewelled) is to aid beauty. They contrast with Muslim women who, if deeply religious, conceal their faces.

The traveller is more likely to pick by dress the religion of an Indian rather than his/her ethnic background. Then again, that dress may reflect the region from which the individual comes, for example the Punjab or Kashmir.

MEETING PEOPLE

Amongst a population of 800 million, you can't help but meet the people and sometimes you would prefer not to be confronted with the many willing and often too insistent residents pressing you to hire, buy or give. If you don't want to do any of these, be very firm in your refusal.

In a country where much poverty abounds, it is natural for travellers to feel threatened or at risk. India is not an easy country to explore because of it. But on the road or rails, in the air and in your accommodations you will find many Indians who are as eager to share conversations and

India and Her People

experiences with a foreigner as you are to discover friendly people with similar aims.

Indians generally are gregarious and warmly eager to impart their knowledge of their history, culture and lifestyles. They are delighted to be greeted in the traditional manner of forming the hands in front of the chest into a near pyramid, as Christians join their hands when saying 'Amen,' This should be accompanied by the Hindi word **'Namaste,'** meaning good morning/afternoon/evening or night.

Perhaps the best way in which to make friends is to wait a few moments when encountering a stranger. If he/she makes no hire/buy/give approaches, it is then up to you to open the conversation. This inevitably produces a friendly response. Indian travellers are invariably polite and helpful as are hotel staffs and tourism officers. While a man will appreciate a westerner's handshake, an Indian woman may feel touch unwelcome. Some may not respond to being addressed by a man, foreigner or local, which is the right of woman of the world - any part. But female foreigner can politely speak to Indian male and, provided she is not provocative in her manner or dress, can expect to be treated with respect. If she is too bare of arm, leg or breast, she can expect to face the consequences she would experience in any other country.

India and Her People

Street scene, Bombay

> **INFOTIP:** Do not be offended if you invite an Indian to join you for a drink that he/she refuses alcohol. It may be against their religion so do offer an alternative.

At times of festival, Hindu in particular, some Indians may spontaneously invite visitors to share their joy of the occasion, even invoking strangers off the street to join them under a marquee for a celebration, such as **Dussehra** (see festivals.) Do not refuse these marvellous opportunities to meet the Indian people at their most exciting and excitable.

> **INFOTIP:** In most restaurants accustomed to western tourists, cutlery is provided. But if you opt to eat by hand Indian-style (which is terrific fun) or are in a restaurant or private home which may not have knives, forks and spoons, do not offend your hosts by eating with the left hand which, traditionally, is used with water for basic toilet cleanliness.

India and Her People

Home stays can be arranged in some Indian cities, giving visitors opportunity to interact with families and understand the Indian way of life. Also some cities, Bombay included, have programmes in which the traveller can meet Indian families in their homes. Contact the Government of India Tourist Office.

INDIAN LANGUAGES

Just as India's population represents a diversity and blending of races, the many languages and dialects used across the great sub-continent are varied. For most visitors using this Info- India, English will be understood by the majority of people they will encounter in the major cities and larger towns. But being able to use even a few words and phrases of the official Indian language **Hindi** is a sure way of expressing true interest and friendship with the Indian people and it can be fun as well. There are many English words used in modern Hindi but in the Roman alphabet their spellings reflect pronunciation with an Indian accent. Example: The English word 'station' would be pronounced as 'steshan' in Hindi. As a guide to approximately correct pronunciation of Hindi words and phrases that follow, the visitor needs to understand Hindi pronunciation of vowels, consonants and diphthons.

a	as in	focal
ar	as in	father
au	as in	laundry
ai	as in	wait
e	as in	they
i	as in	din
ee	as in	feet
o	as in	old
u	as in	put
oo	as in	soon
ch	as in	teach
d	as in	drama
gh	as in	ghost
j	as in	jet
kh	as in	loch
n	as in	French (pronounced nasally)
ph	as in	physical
r	as in	drive
th	as in	think
y	as in	yellow

If the traveller in India leaves the major tourist routes and has trouble being understood by non-English speakers, it

India and Her People

is advisable to ask for the police station as officers in even the smallest centres will have an understanding of English. The Hindi words for police station are **tharnar pulis chowki**. The next most important phrase for visitors to any country is 'Where is a toilet?' With a little bit of luck, you will solve the problem by saying 'Gusalkhana kakan hai?'

A few other useful words and phrases in Hindi are:

man	ardmee
woman	aurat
yes, please	ji, harn
Good morning/afternoon/night	Namaste
Please call a taxi	Kripaya ek taxee bularo
slowly	dheere
stop	ruko
Call a porter please	Portar ko bularo
Show me the menu	Mujhe meenoo kard dikharo
Clean the room	Kamrar sarf karo
The bill, please	Bill laro
May I know your name?	Arpkar shubh narm?
Where is the tourist office?	Toorist arfis kaharn hai?
I want a guide	Mujhe ek garid charhiye
Thank you	Shukriyar
What is the price of this?	Iskee-kyar keemat hai?
Post this letter	Yeh khat leter-baks men darlo
Where is the post and telegraph office?	Dark aur tar ghar kaharn hai?
What is your telephone number?	Apkar telefon nambar?
I am sorry	Mujhe afsos hai
Don't touch this	Ise mat chhuo
Bring the doctor	Daktar ko bularo
What is the time?	Kyar bajar hai?
Where is the bank?	Bank kaharn hai?

Numbers

one	ek	30	tees
two	do	40	charlees
three	teen	50	pachars
four	char	60	sarth
five	parnch	70	sattar
six	chhe	80	assee
seven	sart	90	nabbe
eight	arth	100	sau
nine	nau	1000	hazar
10	das	100,000	larkh
20	bees		

India and Her People

Cremation of a Hindu

HISTORY AND CULTURE

The history of civilization in India spans nearly 5,000 years and only China can similarly boast of an unbroken line in cultural development through such a long period. As with Egypt and Mesapotamia, the annual inundations of India's great rivers produced a richness of soil and an ease of agriculture resulting in a food surplus which is essential to the emergence of an urban-style civilization.

India's earliest urban development dates from about 2,500 BC and, since its discovery in the 1920s, is referred to by archaeologists as the Indus Valley Civilization. Although the two largest cities of Mohenjodaro and Harappa are now in Pakistan, smaller sites have been excavated in the Punjab and the States of Gujarat and Rajasthan, indicating that the civilization was widespread through north west India and what today is eastern Pakistan.

The major excavations have revealed the remains of sophisticated cities and towns laid out on a grid pattern of intersecting streets with clearly defined socio-economic localities as well as public buildings and communal graneries. The **Indus Valley** culture produced artifacts in

India and Her People

copper, bronze, lead and tin and bricks were fired in kilns. These early Indian city dwellers had also developed a pictographic form of writing which so far has defied experts' attempts to translate.

Evidence has emerged that the culture had regular trading relations with the tribal areas of India adjacent to it as well as with other early civilizations such as Sumer in Iraq. These people appear to have had a formalized religion, worshipping both male and female gods. Consistent flooding of the settlements along the Indus river and adjacent to it is believed to have gradually led to a decline in this culture which seemed to have practically disappeared by the time of the first great **Aryan** invasions of India around 1,500 BC.

The *Aryans* were a people originated in central Asia and their hymns, known as the **Vedas**, have been the cornerstone of the Hindu religion. The ancient **Hindus** were a remarkable people who, among other things, are attributed with conceiving the decimal system and algebra. The Aryans were originally cattle-herding, tribal nomads but, in India, they rapidly turned to agriculture, no doubt learned from the remaining people they had conquered, most of whom, it seems, were turned into slaves.

The Indian system of caste can be traced to the Aryan invasions and caste was formally known as varna -literally colour - as a distinction between the fair-skinned Aryans and their darker-complexioned slaves. From this simple division developed class distinctions between the Aryans themselves, resulting in the caste of priests (*Brahmana*,) warriors (*Kshatiya*,) artisans and merchants (*Vaishya*) and farmers (*Shudra*) Later with the refinement of Hinduism came the non-caste of the Untouchable, the lowest of menial workers so reviled that if his shadow touched that of someone of higher status, the latter would have to be cleansed of the contact by ritual.

The Aryan tribes worshipped gods related to the natural elements of sun, water, fire and wind. A milestone in India's civilization occurred in about 1,000 BC with the discovery of iron and the efficiency of the iron axe in creating arable land from forest areas resulted in a rapid growth of population, production and trade.

Another natural result of this development was a constant warring between small communities, resolved as in China, with the emergence of the first empire on the sub-continent. The most famous figure in this **Maurya Empire** was **Ashoka** who ruled from 269 BC to 232 BC. Even before the rise of the **Maurya Dynasty**, India had become aware of the Greek civilization far to the west through the invasion of north-west India by *Alexander the*

Great in 327 BC. Alexander and his armies left a legacy of Macedonian culture and even today the sculpture and art of the areas of the Punjab that he reached have a defineable Greek influence.

The Mauryan empire fell apart soon after the death of Ashoka and India was once again invaded by several peoples out of Asia. At about this time, India's second great empire emerged. Although not as great as the one that had preceded it, the **Gupta dynasty** held sway approximately 200 years and the rulers of this dynasty commenced significant trade with the Greek and Roman civilizations of Europe while a spirit of learning and sophisticated culture spread throughout the empire.

During the same period, the **Chola kingdom** had emerged in what is now the **Tamil Nadu** region of south west India. The Gupta age also saw a flourishing of Hinduism, literature, astronomy, mathematics and drama. But the empire gradually declined and, with it, India's trading links. This led to a greater dependence on rural economy.

Although the soils of India were rich, water had been a constant problem and it was not until the 8th century AD that the development of irrigation, utilizing a geared wheel drawn by oxen, resulted in significant expansion of agricultural production.

Family planning

India and Her People

Fort Aguada Taj, Goa

The 8th century also saw the beginning of Muslim invasions through the north-west passes of India and these incursions - originally more-or-less raids - resulted, over 400 years, in the establishment of Muslim-dominated territories in northern India. The best known of these areas was the **Delhi Sultanate**, the boundaries of which fluctuated quite dramatically the three centuries of its existence.

As the sultanate weakened, northern India represented a glittering prize to any central Asian chieftain with a strong army behind him and the most devastating raid was carried out by **Timur** in 1398. Some 130 years after Timur laid waste to the remaining territories of the Delhi Sultanate, India was again invaded by one of his descendents - the founder of the great **Mughal empire**, **Zahiruddin Mohammad Babur**. Babur's grandson was **Akbar** who extended the **Mughal rule** throughout northern India and a large part of southern India between 1556 and 1605.

Although only a teenager when he ascended the throne, Akbar swiftly improved the bureaucratic and military systems inherited from the days of the Delhi Sultanate and, although illiterate, he patronized religion, art and science. Akbar's reign also saw a blending of both Islamic and Hindu styles of architecture.

The emperor's successors never achieved Akbar's

India and Her People

Indian Fabric detail

grandeur and when, in the 17th century, India witnessed the arrival of the trading adventurers from the major maritime nations of western Europe, the sub-continent was in a state of potential weakness - the traditional open invitation to any conqueror. The first among these newcomers - the Portugese - were quickly followed by Dutch, French and English and the early individual contacts were soon replaced by formalized companies trading in silk, cotton and spices.

By 1707, the great *Mughal empire* had begun to disintegrate into smaller regional sultanates and kingdoms and both the English and French East India companies were alert to exploit this situation while, in turn, fighting among themselves for trade supremacy.

The Europeans were not the only ones to exploit the fragmentation of the empire and, in 1739, the Persian ruler **Nadir Shar** attacked and plundered Delhi, departing with, among other loot, the world famous *Peacock throne* and the *Koh-i-Noor diamond*.

Although the Portugese remained in Goa until after the emergence of modern independent India, the Dutch East India Company withdrew from its early Indian concessions to concentrate on what is today Indonesia. After several decades of intrigue and minor battles, the British outwitted the French interests to emerge as the major western colonizing power.

India and Her People

British power stemmed from the defeat of the ruler of Benghal first in 1757 and again in 1765. By the end of the 18th century, the British East India Company was actively and successfully planning the extension of its rule originally based in the small trading concessions at Madras and Calcutta.

During the first decades of the 19th century, the institution, to be known as the **Raj**, emerged as the British extended their hold and influence over a large part of the sub- continent. By 1857, what had been known as the British empire in India had become known as the British Empire of India.

The exploitation of the British led to ever-mounting resentment among most stratas of Indian society, from the weakened rulers through intellectuals and artisans to the impoverished peasantry. The fuse to this potential powder keg was lit in 1857 by a seemingly minor incident which still epitomized the English indifference to Indian religious and cultural traditions.

The British East India Company had acquired a new type of musket cartridge in which their native troops or sepoys were required to bite a hole before inserting it into the weapon. A rumour was spread that these cartridges were greased with the fat from both cows and pigs. This offended both Muslim and Hindu troops as the Hindus held the cow as sacred and eating of beef as sinful while the

India and Her People

Muslims were forbidden by their religion to touch pork which was considered unclean.

The sepoys at *Meerut* near Delhi rebelled, sparking what has become known as the great Indian mutiny. The Indian troops marched on Delhi where they were joined by other sepoys who had killed their British officers. From Delhi, the revolt rapidly spread throughout northern and central India, engulfing not only soldiers but civiians in towns and villages. The Indians had placed the previously powerless *Mughal emperor* at their head and the resulting fight to the finish was eventually won by the English through superior arms and military tactics and their control over railways and telegraph lines.

Although the mutiny lasted 18 months and produced many Indian heroes and heroines, it culminated in the strengthening of English supremacy in India and a policy of dividing Hindu from Muslim by discriminating against Muslims in many areas of employment. The mutiny also sounded the death-knell of British East India Company power and in 1858, by an act of the British parliament, the administration of all territory in India passed to the British Crown.

Lord Krishna

India and Her People

The mutiny also brought about a fast expansion of the British army in India with far greater emphasis being placed on British rather than native Indian troops and the use of this army to suppress any form of protest against British rule or that of Indian princes whom the English still recognized.

But the dream of a re-emergence of Indian independence was not dead and in 1915, the long road towards it was begun with the return to India from South Africa of one of the 20th century's most remarkable men, **Mohandas Karamchand Gandhi**. Otherwise known as **Mahatma Gandhi**, he, in South Africa, had experienced bitter humiliation over the colour of his skin. He commenced to organize Indian victims of white-British tyranny into a non-violent protest movement. Before Gandhi's real campaign commenced, he embarked on personal journeys throughout most of India's regions, familiarizing himself with the poverty and suffering of the ordinary people.

In 1920, he launched a vast non-cooperation movement which, within two years, saw mass participation throughout India. Both Hindus and Muslims buried their differences in a united struggle against their British masters. By the end of the 1920s, Gandhi had found allies among other Indian nationalists such as **Jawaharlal Nehru** and **Subhash Chandra Bose** and their Indian *Congress Party*.

In 1930, a second wave of civil disobedience began. It was dramatized by Gandhi through one of the most elementary of human needs - salt. The British government had monopolized the manufacture of salt and the revenue received from it and Gandhi set out with his followers on a 250 km walk to the sea on the **Gujarat Coast**, declaring that he would make his own salt and pay no tax. Gandhi was joined along the route by scores of thousands of his fellow Indians, both men and women, from all sections of Indian society. The British met this confrontation quite violently but the atrocities resulted in popular revulsion among the people in Britain and the government called a round- table conference in London where the representatives of several Indian poltical groups were invited to confer on the future of India.

The time was not yet ripe for the British to even contemplate the demands of the Congress Party for Indian independence and, after these London negotiations collapsed, the civil disobedience movement in India began again, defying every form of repression unleashed by the British government.

The progression of the Indian struggle for independence was virtually halted by world war two in Europe then,

India and Her People

despite being one of the victorious allies, the end of six years of conflict saw Great Britain without the military and economic power to continue to suppress the Indian demand for freedom.

Early in 1947, the British government acknowledged the inevitable and the decision to withdraw from India was made. But Britain had made its decision conditional on the partition of the sub-continent to create a new **State of Pakistan**. This was to occupy two regions - one in the west and the other nearly 2,000 km away in Indian territory in what had been **British East Bengal**. The birth of independent India on August 15, 1947 had already been heralded by a tremendous upheaval of religious violence and bloodshed as Hindus within the area to become Pakistan and Muslims within India proper sought to migrate between the two new nations.

It was a bitter experience for the peace-loving Gandhi who, in a small house in Calcutta, wept at the outburst of destruction and death. This, perhaps noblest of all of 20th century humanitarians, was assassinated in January 1948.

Independent India's first Prime Minister was *Jawaharlal Nehru*. He instituted a policy of maintaining not only neutrality for the newly-independent nation but good relationships with Great Britain - which did not endear him to many of his fellow Indians.

Despite Nehru's avowed adherence to Gandhi's philosophy of peaceful confrontation, India was involved in three military confrontations with neighbouring Pakistan in the first 24 years of its independence. Besides these conflicts, triggered by border disputes involving Kashmir and Bangladesh, these first two decades of independence also witnessed military incidents with China. The policy of non-alignment pushed India towards the Soviet Union through American support for Pakistan. Nehru, more commonly known as **Pandit Nehru**, was followed by **Indira Gandhi** until her assassination in 1984 by disgruntled *Sikh* extremists who were members of her personal body-guard. Her son **Rajiv Gandhi** became Prime Minister following her death.

The first 40 or so years of Indian independence has seen the encouragement of foreign investment and increasing industrialization backed during the 1980s with an emphasis on imported technology by the United States, Europe and Japan. The middle class of India has begun to flourish but the nation has not shed inherent difficulties of race and religion epitomized by the struggles of the *Sikhs* in the *Punjab* for an independent identity and the Indian support for the *Tamil* population in neighbouring Sri Lanka.

While supposedly no longer recognized, India's age-old caste system is still an inhibiting factor to efficient national

India and Her People

development and women still struggle for their own independence in a society in which some sections continue to believe in arranged marriages, the dowry system, bride burning and the inevitability of a widow dying on her husband's funeral pyre. For a vast nation which, in the second half of the 20th century, has emerged as the world's most populous western style democracy, India's greatest achievement must be its success in feeding its people while avoiding centralized dictatorships of either the left or the right. Neither the Soviet Union nor the People's Republic of China have succeeded in this common goal.

Slowly but surely, India's policy of industrial modernization has placed it in 10th position of the industrialized nations of the world.

Indian Sculpture

India and Her People

INDIA'S GLORIOUS ARCHITECTURE

One only has to drive through the villages and observe the manner in which the Indian women style cow pats into neat, visually attractive structures drying for future use as fuel or fertilizer, to realize how inherent is the artistry of construction within the souls of the people. The cow pats and also the haystacks of varied sizes and shapes that draw the visitor from a vehicle to photograph against a backdrop of clear sky and scenic interest, are works of art.

Mahatma Gandhi's Home

India and Her People

India's architecture, as impermanent as a haystack and a shrine-like stack of cow pats, or as enduring as the *Taj Mahal*, is as much a reflection of its people's creativity as its history and religions. The visitor to India will inevitably be exposed to the architecture of at least two millenia and an understanding of the development of India's unique buildings is essential to its appreciation. The traditions stretch back to the mists of pre-history and the great **Indus Valley Civilization** where both sun-dried and fired bricks were used to create quite sophisticated private and communal structures in the large cities of *Harappa, Mohenjodaro, Lothal* and *Kalibangan*.

The technique of the arch had been mastered by these ancient people and the excavation of the **Great Bath** at Mohenjodaro is proof that ritualistic public buildings had been created at that time. This first flowering of practical and decorative architecture was swept away into a dark age that followed the Aryan invasions and, for nearly 2,000 years, Indian building and architecture languished in simple structures of circular huts with domed roofs until the medium of stone suddenly appeared in the third and second centuries BC.

Stone buildings have been linked with the emergence of the Buddhist religion and many of the earliest examples have survived until the present day. The first use of stone centred around the building of the stupa or funerary mound and progressed to a hall of worship and then a monastery. The earliest examples show a reflection in stone of the wooden structures that preceded them. Early Buddhist architecture frequently was created around natural caves where large prayer halls were excavated and the monk/architects introduced stone carvings to pillars and rafters.

In the centuries that followed, a tremendous expansion and diversity occured in religious architecture, principally under the great *Gupta dynasty* and even recently-built Hindu temples still bear the influence of this period. During these centuries, the temple evolved from the simple square chamber that existed in early Gupta shrines in central India to quite elaborate structures and, in the later Gupta period, there emerged the temple spire that became the characteristic feature of Hindu temple architecture. It appeared in two forms. In the north, it was known as the *shikhara* and was smoothly pyramidal, rising to a rounded top with a pointed tip. In the south, the spire, known as the *vimana*, soared in a series of diminishing steps, similar to the stepped pyramids of early Egypt and Mexico.

The earliest of these spires were evident in the 6th century temples in what is now the **State of Karnataka** but their final peak of refinement came at **Mahabalipuram**

India and Her People

near **Madras** in the 8th century where they were fashioned from outcrops of rock. The temple architecture was further refined between the 10th and 13th centuries and the finest examples of this era are found at **Khajuraho** in central India, where the sculptures to be seen today are incredibly erotic, **Thanjavur** in the south and at **Konarak** in the east. Intricate carvings covering these remarkable buildings were reflections of the life of the people. At **Tamil Nadu**, vestibules called gudha mandapas and towering gateways known as gopurams became part of temple design.

During the Hoysala dynasty from the 11th to the 14th century, the northern and southern styles blended and the form of the shikhara and the vimana were amalgamated into a bell-shaped tower above a star-shaped shrine. The temple facades were richly decorated with sculptures of gods and their consorts.

Early Muslim invaders of India had no influence on traditional Hindu architecture but, after the 13th century and the first Muslim conquest, a new tradition of building began to emerge. An early Muslim king, **Qutb-ud-din Aibak** who became ruler of Delhi, commanded to be built the first mosque in India. His architects wrecked existing Hindu and Jain temples for the raw material of this mosque which was a hotch potch of design and building expediency between the Muslim overseers and their subjugated Hindu stone masons.

The subsequent history of Muslim architecture in India is a story of gradual fusion of two opposite religious ideals into the richest period of design and construction. Most of the monumental buildings over the next 500 years were memorials to the vanity of rulers and, with the establishment of the **Mughal empire**, an era of unparalleled building activity commenced. Architects and artisans from every part of India were given free reign to express their ideas in stone and the resulting mixture of both Hindu and Muslim styles were many and varied.

Most buildings during Akbar's long reign were constructed of sandstone but his son **Jahangir** preferred the lustre of pure white marble although he was not an outstanding builder and liked to express his creativity in the laying out of Moghul gardens. Jahangir's successor, **Shahjahan** renewed the Moghul building frenzy and took the traditions of Moghul architecture to their climactic best in the famous **Taj Mahal at Agra**. Shahjahan was responsible for the city of **Shahjahanabad** at Delhi and, in the seraglio (harem building,) there is a profusion of luxuriously embellished marble pavilions surrounded by gardens and water channels. Shahjahan's son, **Aurangzeb** ruled the slowly disintegrating Moghul empire for 60 years

India and Her People

during which period no great work of architecture was created.

The coming of the British to India put an effective end to indigenous Indian architecture with the invaders' determination to erect uncompromising copies of Greek, Renaissance and Gothic buildings created from plans and sketches imported from England. To a lesser extent, the Portugese, French and Dutch reflected the architecture of their homelands on the buildings they erected in India. While some of these monumental edifaces were almost grudgingly embellished with motifs from the Indian traditions, the basic forms were definitely western.

When India achieved independence in 1947, Prime Minister Nehru called for the development of a truly Indian architecture but the first attempts by the new nation's designers were somewhat awkward imitations of the past. Nehru insisted on a new and vital style of contemporary architecture and commissioned the Frenchman, *Corbusier*, to build a capital city for the new State of the Punjab at *Chandigarh*.

Corbusier planned the city in a scheme of integrated sectors and introduced to visual expression the forms of raw concrete and his now-famous bries soleil or sun breakers which shaded windows from a number of angles. The renowned Frenchman set the pattern for what is now recognized as modern Indian architecture, laying great stress on functionalism and economy.

Currently architecture is in a state of flux throughout India. In many regions, architects are recognising the great importance of local conditions and are creating buildings that, while utilitarian, pose no threat to the aesthetics of their environment.

PART II
Sightseeing

Snake Chamber

BOMBAY, GATEWAY OF INDIA

Most modern and cosmopolitan of all India's cities, Bombay is sometimes termed the New York of the East because of its skyscrapers and the glamour and pace of its urban life. More visitors disembark at this bustling, seething port city than anywhere else. Its most famed landmark is the **Gateway of India** which was built in honour of England's King George V's arrival in Bombay in 1911. But the city is a gateway also in that it is the buffer which helps the westerner adjust to the culture and mores of the intriguing sub-continent.

Built on a cluster of islands which, originally were home to aboriginal fisherfolk, Bombay is located just short of half way up the continent, west on the Arabian Sea.

On the largest of its islands, the early inhabitants built a shrine to the goddess **Mumbadevi** and the place became known as **Mumbai**. Now the islands, all united, retain their names only as districts - *Mahim, Mazgaon, Parel, Worli, Colaba, Girgaum* and *Colaba* and added to them has been land reclaimed by the sea - *Churchgate* and *Nariman Point*.

Capital of the **State of Maharashtra**, Bombay is western India's only national deep water harbour and its port is one of the world's busiest, having come into its own following the 19th century opening of the **Suez Canal**. It is India's commercial capital, paying one third of the nation's income tax. It has the world's largest cloth market and is the centre of the largest motion picture industry on earth.

You can visit a studio or a set to see part of one of about 600 full feature movies shot in Bombay each year being made. These are quite star-studded productions, even though the stars might be involved in several roles for different films simultaneously. The Government of India Tourist Office keeps its fingers on the production pulse and can arrange a visit by request.

Bombay never sleeps. It pulsates with people, the millions of commuters who pour in from the suburbs and out daily by train, bus, taxi and car to work, and the estimated 500 villagers who arrive weekly from the countryside in search of employment, boosting the city's nine million population to a density four times that of New York.

For centuries, Bombay was rather a drab city, unchanged from the time its seven marshy islands were settled by the fisherpeople. It was given to the Portugese by **Sultan Bahadur Shah** of *Gujarat* and, for just over 500 rupees, was bought by physician and botanist **Dr. Garcia da Orta** in 1549. Several substantial churches were built.

Bombay

Then it grew after the Portugese gifted it to the British as part of the dowry of *Catherine de Braganza* on her marriage to Charles II. Given to the East India Company in 1668, Bombay was introduced to law and order the following year by its governor, **Gerald Augier** and with it came a judiciary, mint, better fortifications, town planning and building of houses and a hospital. When the *Surat* ship-building yard was moved to Bombay, it was a major turning point for the port. *Sir Bartle Frere*, governor from 1862 to 1867, initiated more growth and the expansion of the cotton industry also signalled more development in road and rail communications.

Britain fused Bombay's islands and left a legacy of neo-Gothic and arcaded buildings. More land was reclaimed from the sea to extend the slipper-shaped united island in the sea but room for its increasing population remains a problem and the only means of expansion has been up. For a long time, the city suffered from a lack of greenery because of this development but in recent years, there has been concerted effort to plant more trees and shrubs and the results have begun to show.

Bombay's appeal is its contrasts - the glittering hotels and limousines blending into a village atmosphere of mud huts, old temples and horse-drawn carts with jingling bells; the fabulous shops and emporia tempting the shopper with India's exotic wares as easily as the crowded mazes of timeless, colourful bazaars; its people in well-cut western clothing mingling with those wearing garments unchanged in design for centuries. This results from the mix of *Maharashtrians, Gujarats*, north and south *Indians, Goans* and *Parsis* in the one, sometimes aggressive city.

Arriving by air at night, one sees **Marine Drive** *sparkling below beside the Arabian Sea* and living up to its other name, The **Queen's Necklace**. There are jewels of experience to be found in the world's seventh largest city. It throbs ceaselessly with vitality.

Discovering Fort Bombay and the South, Gateway of India

The logical place in which to start an exploration of this teeming city is in its south east at the place every visitor associates with the image of Bombay, the Gateway of India. This is the first landmark which will be seen by travellers arriving into the harbour by ship. There is little of the fortification by colonials left in Bombay because former governor Sir Bartle Frere tore down the walls of the old fort to make way for city expansion. But the area still retains its name and it is easy to divide the city into three for the purposes of your easy orientation - Fort Bombay (which

Bombay

we combine with South Bombay) central Bombay and suburban (north) Bombay.

Conceived in 1911 to commemorate the visit to India of King George V and Queen Mary of England, the Gateway of India was originally a temporary arch of plaster, hastily erected in time for the couple's farewell after a five-week stay in India. The ochre basalt, 26 metre arch as seen now was completed in 1924. Entered from four archways, it is comprised of a square within a rectangle with four domed turrets on top and was designed by *George Wittett* in the 16th century style of the neighbouring *State of Gujurat*. It has been described as a combination of the Arc de Triomphe and part of a Moorish Palace. Next to the monument and rather overshadowed is an equestrian statue of **Chatrapati Shivaji**, the greatest of the **Maratha people**, who made some raids on the occupying British but ultimately lost his territory to them. The 17th century hero had defied the Moghuls to establish his own kingdom. There is also a statue of **Swami Vivekananda**

After passing through the Gateway of India, which is a very popular meeting place for locals, one descends down steps to a landing stage where launches and small ferries (with guide) and smaller boats (without guide) leave for **Elephanta Island** and its temple caves. The vessels sans guide are naturally cheaper. The island is one of Bombay's major attractions. From the Gateway too,tourists can take a boat for a 15 minute cruise around the harbour and a sailor's eye view of the monument.

Bombay's tallest building

Bombay

Times are a bit vague for Elephanta and harbour trips. When the vessel fills with passengers, it leaves.

If you are into nautical history, you go by boat to the **Maritime Museum** on **Battery Island** which is just off the Gateway of India. The museum is the only one of its kind in India, located on what is called **'Middle Ground'**. It has memorabilia which traces back India's ocean-going heritage from the period of Alexander the Great. It includes plates and crests used by the great Maratha seafarers and models of legendary ships. A complete section is also set aside for Lord Louis Mountbatten.

The museum is open only on weekends and public holidays and private and government launches and boats will transport visitors there at regular intervals. Inquire at Gateway of India.

The Elephanta Caves

The 10 kilometre, 45 to 60 minute voyage to Elephanta can be taken from 9 am to 2.30 pm daily with the exception of the monsoon season, June to September. As there is no accommodation on the island, you should watch the time in this green, treed place if you are not to miss the return boat. This can be an economical day excursion in which you can walk many trails on the island in addition to visiting the cave temples. But if you are in a hurry, you can be back at the Gateway of India by lunchtime.

From the ferry, you will see fishing boats under sail, tankers approaching to disgorge their oil at **Butcher Island** to be transported to Bombay refineries and the electricity plant and atomic energy institute.

Just before arrival on the island, visitors transfer to **dhows** which are shallow-drafted enough to reach the narrow wharf. Walking along it, you will pass fisher-women balancing copper and brass pots on their heads. The track ascends then there are 140 steps to the cave temples.

INFOTIP: If the day is hot, you might be tempted to accept the many offers of ' Chair. Chair.' The Maharajah-style chairs are carried up the steps by four bearers and back, although you can descend on foot if you wish. Just make sure you establish the price of the ride before sitting down.

Originally called **Gharapuri**, or the fortress city, the island was renamed by the Portugese after a big stone elephant statue near the wharf which collapsed in 1814. It

Bombay

was later moved to **Victoria Gardens** in Bombay and reassembled.

While the temples are believed by some authorities to have been carved in the 6th century by Hindu *Rashtrakuta* kings in line with the earlier revival of Hinduism, others maintain their origins are unknown and that they date from the 7th century. Carved out of rocks between two hills, they are in praise of the god of destruction, *Shiva, Shivaism* essentially being worship of the phallus. Until a few centuries ago, this was a flourishing place of worship although believers in small numbers still come to Elephanta.

The main cave temple is 130 foot-square, supported by massive pillars on square bases with fluted shafts. Its columned entrance is guarded by elephant sculptures. Doorkeepers (**dwarapala**) are carved from pillars at each end of the facade. You will find the major sculptures on the rear wall. Dwarapalas are in three square recesses. Shiva is represented in both male and female forms on a left panel while he is depicted with his love **Parvati** on the right. Dominating the central hall is Shiva as the 18-foot high triple-imaged **Great Lord Maheswanti**, his faces depicting the Hindu Trinity of Brahma, the creator, Shiva, the destroyer and, between them, *Vishnu*, the preserver.

The main cave temple bears striking resemblance to the **Dumar Lona Cave** at **Ellora**. Shiva is shown bringing the river **Ganges** down to earth and, seated on a lotus, becomes lord of yogis - **Yogisvara**. In another panel, he has sprouted many arms to become **Nataraja**, the universal dancer. The beautiful power of the sculptures transports the visitor to a time when the strength of human faith could achieve almost the artistically impossible. There's a small admission charge to the caves but on Fridays entry is free.

> **INFOTIP:** Most visitors make Elephanta a four-hour trip. While there are tea and bottled soft drinks stalls and a snack stall near the caves, also drinks available on the boat, bring a picnic lunch if you intend to make a day of it. It is very crowded on weekends.

As you return to Bombay harbour and the Apollo Bunder, the road in front of it, the **Taj Mahal Hotel** will appear behind the Gateway. It is almost a monument in itself, having been described by the Times of London in 1903 as '*the finest caravanserai in the East.*' Today, it is rated as among the world's 10 best hotels. Stroll into its public rooms and restaurants for a glimpse of the era of the British Raj. The hotel has an art gallery with weekly exhib-

Bombay

itions of paintings and sculptures and it also holds varied cultural performances.

There is a legend that the French architect who designed this magnificent building of granite staircases and 400 rooms with ceiling fans (innovative for its day,) holidayed in France while the hotel was being constructed. On his return, he discovered it had been built back to front and not facing the waterfront. The legend says that such was his dismay, he suicided from a top floor.

Also on the Apollo Bunder is the Royal Bombay Yacht Club. A magnificent building founded in 1880, it was a preserve of the British until independence and houses one of Bombay's finest bars and a fascinating collection of trophies.

After walking along *Rajkavi Bhushan Marg* (Landsdown Road,) you will then enter an intersection of six roads at *Shyama Prasad Mukharji Chowk*. The imposing **Maharashtra Police** headquarters are on one corner to the right, should you ever need them and, directly ahead is the Prince of Wales Museum on Mahatma Gandhi Road.

Thieve's Market, Chor Bazaar

Bombay

The Prince of Wales Museum

Also built to commemorate the 1911 visit of the Prince and Princess of Wales, this white-domed structure of Indo-Saracenic style was opened to the public in 1923. The dome was modelled on the famed **Gol Gumbaz** in Bijapur and its large gardens, bright with bougainvillea, are dotted with bronze Chinese statues. One of India's largest musea and Bombay's finest, the Prince of Wales museum houses a massive collection of art drawn from all parts of the country. Some are as venerable as 10 centuries old. The three major sections focus on art, archaeology and natural history but there are also excellent textile, war equipment and armament and ivory exhibits. There are substantial Nepalese art and coin collections also.

Most prized of the collections are the *Deccan* and *Rajasthani* early miniatures, regarded as the finest in the world. The museum is open every day except Monday and, on Tuesday, admission is free.

Bombay

Jehangir Art Gallery

In the same grounds is the prominent Jehangir Art Gallery, not to be confused with the Jehangir Nicholson Museum of Modern Art which is east on Nariman point in the National Centre for Performing Arts. The former is a centre of changing, essentially contemporary exhibitions with up to four being held simultaneously. State-level exhibitions and symposia are held here and there is a good adjoining library.

This gallery also has a snack bar, toilets and telephones. Bombay has the biggest representation of modern art in India. The swell began in the 1940s when Lord Louis Mountbatten sought to make Italian prisoners of world war II, (transported to Bombay because of lack of space in Europe,) work for their maintenance. Recalling the great traditions of Italian art, he directed talented prisoners to paint. Their modern works became immensely popular and an era was begun, particular when many of India's prominent painters achieved fame in Bombay.

> **INFOTIP:** Because of its artistic reputation, Bombay has spawned hundreds of establishments purporting to be art galleries when they are outlets for jewellery, souvenirs garments etc. These are still fun to enter but if you are on the genuine hunt for art works to appreciate or to buy, consult the art gallery directory towards the end of this book.

Opposite the Jehangir Art Gallery on Rampart Row (or 34 K, Dubash Marg,) is the **Chetana Restaurant** which serves very good, economical vegetarian, Rajasthani and Gujurati food thali style. A rear door opens up to a bookshop specialising in Indian philosophies and religions (English titles available,) and next-door, the craft shop of the same name has quality replicas of antique brass figures, puppets, designer clothes and other interesting items. In the same street is the Copper Chimney which is slightly down at heel in appearance but prepares top Tandoori food. It's particular popular with foreigners in the know.

Bombay University and Rajabai Clock Tower

On the left along Mahatma Gandhi Road, opposite the museum are buildings which include that of the Army and Navy. Then you will come to the handsome Bombay University, a series of buildings built in 1874 and characterised by Venetian galleries and open staircases.

Victoria Station, Bombay

The garden is very pleasant and, for an experience of a hallowed hall of learning, you are welcome to wander in the grounds. Most fanous of the University buildings is the **Rajabai Clock Tower** which also houses the institution's library. Five storeys high, it ascends 260 feet. It has eight statues on the way up and at the top of the tower are 16 more. In the old days of British occupation, the clock on the fifth storey used to play Rule Brittania, God Save the King, Auld Lang Syne and a Handel Symphony among 16 tunes which changed four times a day. Today, the clock tells only the time.

You need permission to climb the tower but if you gain it, you will be rewarded with a view of the High Court building just beyond, with its statues of Mercy and Justice.

Bombay

Street market

Flora Fountain

Continuing along Mahatma Gandhi Road, you will come to **Hutatma Chowk**, one of Bombay's busiest intersections. In the centre is another monument to British colonialism, formerly known as the Flora Fountain. It was built in 1869 with assistance from a rich Bombay merchant who wished to honour the governor of the day, Sir Bartle Frere. On one side, it is bordered by a car park but on the other is a monument to the victims of riots during the agitation for a separate *State of Maharashtra* in the 1950s.

The goddess Flora is atop the fountain which is now maintained privately by the city department stores Akbararallys. It is still a popular site for rallies and meetings. Hutatma Chowk, which means **Martyr's Square**, is Bombay's business centre, circled by banks, offices, shops and colleges. View it on Sundays for a distinctly slower change of pace. Flora Fountain has been likened to London's Picadilly Circus.

Bombay

Horniman Circle

Turn right into Veer Nariman Road towards Horniman Circle which is also a business and shopping area. On the right is St Thomas Cathedral. This is one of the oldest Christian churches in west India with a history dating back to 1672 when it was planned by the Governor of Bombay, Gerald Augier. While the foundation stone was laid in 1676, insufficient funds meant work had to be postponed for several years. The church was completed in 1718, consecrated in 1816 and its ornate facade is as when first completed. There are distinctive stained glass windows and brass plaques and marble statuary line the walls. The chairs in which King George V and Queen Mary sat during their 1911 visit still remain and the church is open for worship.

Walk east and through **Horniman Circle** and you will face the old **Town Hall** housing the **Royal Asiatic Society Library** which is among the oldest and largest libraries in India. Inside are many commanding statues of colonial rulers and past local philanthropists. Next door is the the **Mint** which dates back to 1829. Permission to visit must be gained from the Mint Master. Just south of the library is the **Old Customs House** built in 1720. From the Mint, head north along Mint Road and at its end is the general Post Office, just east of another large intersection known as Nagar Chowk.

Victoria Railway Terminus

Follow Dadabhai Navroji Marg (or road) north and you won't fail to miss the massive Victoria Railway Terminus. It is known to locals and on some maps as VT. Built in 1888 of Porbander sandstone and Malad trapstone, it is regarded as the city's most beautiful building. A combination of Indian and Gothic architecture, its exterior traces the history of the evolution of transport in India and prosperity and progress is reflected in ornate figures. It was designed by *Frederick William Stevenson* and is next to the Central Railway headquarters. and from it, Bombay's first railway line stretched about 35 km to **Thana**.

All over the station, gargoyles are surrounded by friezes of snakes, monkeys, rats and peacocks and the entrance gate is attended by two huge statues - a lion and a tiger. Miss Progress, holding a spoked wheel in her left hand and a torch in her right is the statue which stands on top of the high main dome.

Bombay

In and out of the impressive main entrance flows a proportion of the three million people who arrive and depart on 1000 trains daily. This is not a station in which to become separated from travel companions. It is one of the world's most crowded.

Bombay Municipal Corporation

The Bombay Municipal Corporation, just opposite VT, is domed with a central staircase and has minarets and a statue of *Sir Phirozshah Mehta* in its foreground. It is another fine example of Saracenic-Gothic architecture by Stevenson and its dome is 71.5 metres high.

From Nagar Chowk, retrace your steps down Dadabhai Navroji Marg, which is an interesting shopping street, until you reach its intersection with Mahatma Gandhi and Veer Nariman Roads. Take a short stroll north up Mahatma Gandhi until the **Bombay Gymkana** comes into view. This is a large area of parkland where sports including rugby and tennis are played.

The attraction of the left will already have caught your eye. It is a dazzling length of open air stalls, all displaying and selling western clothing. The garments for men, women and children have all been manufactured for the western market but because of small flaws, a wrong sizing affixed, a caught thread etc., these have been rejected for export. There are some marvellous bargains to be had here and bargain you will. It's lots of fun. Trace your steps back to Veer Narriman and turn right.

For another, fascinating deviation, double back north just a little way again at Maharishi Karvi Road. On the right is

Portuguese style resort, Goa

Bombay

the central *Government of India Tourist Office* which will assist you with maps, literature and planning the rest of your stay in India if it's not already done. Adjacent is the railway booking office. On the left, almost directly opposite, is the Churchgate Railway station built in 1890.

It is here, at lunchtimes from noon to about 2.30 pm weekdays that you will see a happening rarely observed by tourists. Bombayites are very fond of their homecooked food and have a system called dabawala of transporting their hot lunches to the office or schools of their children. Food is kept hot in metal containers called **tiffins** and, each work day, the tiffin men in ox or horse-drawn carts or bicycles with addendums collect the containers from the houses and apartments and take them to the nearest railway station.

The colour-coded containers arrive at VT, Bombay Central and other stations, which include Churchgate, to be distributed in the city by more tiffin men and the empty containers are subsequently returned, continue by rail then to the residence of origin. It's an amazing system which, logicistically, should not work but it does and watching the unloading and return of the tiffins is unusual entertainment.

Another facet of life is the collection of laundry from residences by the **dhobi carts**. People pay for the laundering of about 100 items at a time. These are taken to open air laundries where they are washed on stone or cement and dried in the sun in the manner of centuries. Be on the lookout for several such colourfully busy laundries in the city. Despite the millions of clothing articles and tiffins, few are ever mislaid.

Bombay

Nariman Point

Veer Nariman is the location of the centrally located Ambassador Hotel although its official address is Churchgate. This four-star establishment has a top floor revolving restaurant featuring French, Continental and Indian food. Veer Nariman heads west to Back Bay and Marine Drive (at night The Queen's Nacklace) which is also named Netaji Subhash Road.

Proceeding south along Marine Drive, characterized by its modern skyscrapers, you'll find **Air India** and **Indian Airlines** in the same building on the corner of Madam Cama Road.

Ahead, almost on Nariman Point is Bombay's tallest building, the **Oberoi Towers Hotel** which has recently been joined next door by the new Oberoi Hotel. The latter has an enormous atrium lobby which could be compared with the Hanging Gardens of Babylon if one could imagine what they had been like. Here is a most elegant place to take tea in the afternoon or a drink in the evening. The two hotels are internally connected. Between them are nine excellent restaurants.

One is The Moghul Room where authentic frontier food is served to the strains of live classical Indian music with dancers. Next door, the Oberoi's Kandahar Restaurant's succulent tandoori fare is eaten by hand (right only, please,) and the chefs can be seen cooking behind glass. On the Oberoi Towers' 35th floor, the intimate bar and lounge is popular with foreign guests for its piano entertainment and top of Bombay view.

On the tip of Nariman Point is the **National Centre for Performing Arts**, a contemporary-styled but elegant building including the Tata Theatre. Designed by Philip Jonson, it was opened in 1981. Its deep lobby is bordered by stone on one side and the gigantic murals of *Shiavax Chavda* on the other make for a dramatic result. A spectacular staircase leads to the main auditorium which accommodates 1040 people. The elegant Tata Theatre features crystal chandeliers. With ultra modern sound and lighting equipment, the centre is favoured as a venue for performers of international acclaim, particularly in winter.

The centre is also home to the **Jehangir Nicholson Museum** of Modern Art, named after Jehangir Nicholson's massive collection of works housed in the permanent gallery. The works of some of India's most renowned artists are exhibited. These include Bikash Bhattacharee, Husain, Krishen Khanna, Laxman Shreshta, Mohan Samant and N.S. Bendre.

Bombay

Overloaded rickshaw

Afghan Church

It's quite a hike to walk further south from this point to the Afghan Church via **Colaba Village** where **Koli** fisherfolk live on the beach among their traditional vessels against a backdrop of skyscrapers. Similarly, you might need to reorientate yourself at the Victoria Terminus and proceed south through streets, including the Colaba Causeway, including the **Colaba market**.

This four-kilometre long area of stalls and shops sells absolutely everything and offers the city's widest and most surprising choices. In the Colaba area, you'll find many of Bombay's budget accommodations, a crazy combination of foreign- style el cheapo eateries and some amazing characters.

Because the southern tip of Bombay is also populated by naval and army personnel, some of the area is restricted so best bet is to take a cab. Stop on the way to observe the Kolis. (No, this is not a typographical error. They are the Koli people from Colaba.) These people speak **Maratha**, the original language and are descendents of one of the original fishing tribes. The women are proud, wear their saris drawn tightly between their legs Marathi style and stride purposefully, selling their fish all over the city, their hair slicked back and interwoven with flowers. Their dance is distinctive so do try to catch it at a cultural show in hotel or theatre. The children are very friendly and love to be photographed.

Bombay

Outdoor food stalls

In Colaba too, you may see some of the millions of Bombay's articles of laundry drying in the sea air and smell fish drying as well. On the former *Colaba Island*, the bougainvillea sways in the wind in brilliant profusion.

Set amid greenery off Dr. Nanabai Moos Marg, the Catholic St. John's Church is also known as the Afghan Church because it commemorates the British who fell in the Sind and Afghan campaigns of 1838 and 1843. The gothic church was built in 1847 and its spire can be seen from quite some distance away. On the return north, go via Cuffe Parade and turn left at G.D. Somani Marg. On the corner is the President Hotel which, in addition to having Italian and Indian restaurants, the latter with live entertainment, also houses Bombay's only Thai restaurant.

> **INFOTIP:** Do not photograph buildings in the restricted military area. Photography is not permitted at airports. Special permission from the Archaeological Survey, Sion Fort Bombay is needed for professional photographers with tripods and flash to photograph protected monuments.

Bombay

World Trade Centre

Turn left at the next intersection and you will see the World Trade Centre. This is a complex of banks, investment and trading companies, textile outlets, travel companies, shops and State Government emporia of *Mysor, Punjab, Madhya Pradesh, Jammu* and *Kashmir, Uttar Pradesh, Himachal Pradesh* and the State of which Bombay is capital, *Maharashtra*. If you are not visiting other States, here you will find crafts, furniture, carpets and other articles from the places of origin at fixed prices. There are camera, photocopying and computer maintenance services, a post office and canteen.

CENTRAL BOMBAY

Temples and Traffic

For a moment, let's return to Marine Drive from Nariman Point and explore sweeping **Back Bay** before heading inland again and proceeding further north. As mentioned before, the drive which stretches between the point and **Malabar Hill**, (from which its jewelled beauty is best appreciated at night,) is an evening must be seen when it is illuminated and romantic. Once though, it was likened to pearls but now that the drive is bathed in more saffron-like light, one could say the Queen's Necklace was made of amber. If you walk it, (though it's a long thoroughfare) there are numerous stalls selling soft drinks along the promenade. During the monsoon season, the sea can become quite rough - which accounts for the drive's protective, yet low wall. The promenade area was reclaimed from the sea in 1920.

Taraporewala Aquarium

Heading north, on the right you will see the various gymkanas or sports clubs of different Bombay groups - Parsis, Islam, Wilson College, Grant Medical College, the Bombay City Police playground and the Catholic gymkana. The latter is next to the Taraporewala Aquarium which was opened in 1951 and has an interesting population of both fresh and sea water fish. Water is piped from Back Bay for the marine fish. Fishery by-products, shells and articles crafted from shells are also displayed. The aquarium is open between 11 am and 8 pm Tuesday to Saturday and 10 am to 8 pm Sundays. It is closed Monday.

Bombay

Basilica of the Born Jesus

Chowpatty Beach

The aquarium is just south of **Chowpatty Beach**. Too polluted for swimming and by no means comparable to Bombay's better beaches, Chowpatty remains an exciting place to visit, particularly in late afternoon and evening. Scene of mass political demonstrations during the struggle for freedom, the beach still occupies a special place in the lives and hearts of Bombayites. It is here, by the statue of the 20th century political leader **Tilak**, that political meetings are still held, along with special festivals including the early September celebration of **Ganesh Chaturthi**. On this day the elephant god Ganesh is revered and millions of people bring their own statues of Ganesh to brandish while the bigger effigies are paraded in large processions.

Coconut Day in August is another exciting time to visit. The day marks the end of the monsoon and the fisherfolk and their friends go down to the sea to offer coconuts to satisfy the sea gods. Then those who earn their livings from the sea, put out to it immediately. On the beach any day could be found acrobats, jugglers, sculptors fashioning gods and popular celebrities out of sand and holymen burying themselves beneath it. There are inevitably pedlars and, especially in the evenings, people congregate to enjoy Bombay's specialty snacks and ice cream from the scores of *Bombaywallahs* at their lit stalls.

Bombay

The most famous of the vendors is the *Bhelpuriwalla* who sells spicy puffed rice and chutney with tiny pancakes called puri. The *Chanasingwalla* offers gram and peanuts in pointed cones. From the *Narialpaniwalla*, you can buy coconuts pierced with a straw, sugar cane from the *Gannewalla* and icecream from the *Kulfiwalla* - if you are sure your stomach will not react adversely to it. It would be wiser to give the ice cream a miss. For your fortune to be told, consult the *Jyotishwalla* but be a little wary of the *Talmalishwalla*. His role is to give oil massages.

Malabar Hill

Sweeping right round the bay and rising up Malabar Hill, the road becomes Walkeshwar Road. Take a cab as the distance from Chowpatty Beach is quite far. The hill is topped by the **Kamala Nehru Park** which was landscaped in 1952 as a children's park named after the wife of India's first Prime Minister Nehru. It has a magnificent view of Back Bay and Marine Drive and is located on B.D.Kher Road. But first on the road sharing the name of Walkeshwar district, you will pass by some of Bombay's most valuable real estate. This is mainly a **Gujurati** neighbourhood and you will identify the women by their saris which hang down over their right shoulders. The Gujuratis tend to dominate Bombay's trade and have reaped the rewards.

Bombay

Jain Temple

On the right of the same road is the Jain Temple. Dedicated to **Tirthankara** or the Jain religion's first apostle, the shrine of the marble temple built in 1904 is flanked on the walls by bright paintings which retrace various events in the lives of this faith's 24 Tirthankaras. The first floor has a special shrine carved out of black marble and dedicated to **Parsvanath**. On the ceiling are planets as personified in the Hindu religion.

There are two more interesting temples in this area, the **Raj Bhavan** on the same road, almost on the tip of Malabar Point and the Walkeshwar Temple which is near the rear entrance of the Raj Bhavan. The latter is in ruins, having been built between 810 and 1260 AD.

> **INFOTIP:** In all temples and mosques in India, (non-functioning ruins being the exception,) the visitor must remove his shoes. Often these are minded by a person at the entrance. It is customary to give a tip when claiming your shoes - about one rupee. Also, if places of worship are on your agenda, women should dress modestly and not offend the sensibilities of the people. Wear flat-heeled shoes. Temples and mosques usually mean steps, often many of them.

> **INFOTIP:** Both men and women carrying leather purses or wearing leather moneybelts may be refused entry to some Jain and Hindu temples in line with their non-violent religious philosophies. You would not want to leave your money and valuables outside the temples so if you know they are on the agenda, carry a cotton, plastic or straw carryall and, men, conceal your wallets.

Hanging Gardens

If you continue as far as Malabar Point, the first major left hand fork in the road will be **Bal Gangadhar** (or B.G. Kher Marg.) The children's park with some amusements - and always plenty of hawkers and stalls outside - is now on the right while the famed Hanging Gardens are on your left. In this area, you will have seen the leafy green camouflage, at least, bordering Government House. The high, Hanging Gardens face west and the Arabian Sea as well as the city to the east.

Known as **Pherozeshah Mehta Gardens**, this extensive park was laid out far ahead of the children's park below. Landscaped on top of the reservoir which supplies many areas of Bombay with water, the Hanging Gardens began to provide Bombayites with cool relief and green aspects

Shaha Shahouri Mosque

Bombay

above hot city streets from 1881. The hedges of the gardens have been manicured into animal shapes and there is an unusual flower clock to be seen. Sunsets from the gardens provide magnificent spectacle.

Continuing north along B.D. Kher Marg, you will pass on your left an enclosure with distant high-walled buildings which you might admire for its trees and creepers then dismiss unless you are aware that these are the **Parsi Towers of Silence**. Look to the sky and wheeling carrion birds might tell part of the story.

Here is a place of the dead. Parsi mourners are admitted to the enclosure but can only go so far to grieve and meditate. The visitor cannot expect more than to be a street passer-by. When a Parsi dies in Bombay, his body is taken to this place and transported by bearers to a tower where the body is placed in the open air on a grid, free to the vultures above. Any remaining bones, after a few days, drop into pits of charcoal and lime and are thence washed into the sea unpolluted.

The Parsis, descendants of Persia, are against pollution and for natural preservation, hence the encouragement of the birds. There are two Parsi philosophies behind this practice. They are derived from the *Zoroastrian* faith which reveres life on earth too much to pollute it. Fire, water and earth are sacred to the Parsis. The second philosopby is that rich and poor, in death, are the same and, then, should be the equal.

Hanuman, the Monkey God

Bombay

Crawford Market

Mani Bhavan
(Mahatma Gandhi Memorial Museum)

It is a bit of a winding diversion east to locate the home where Mahatma Gandhi stayed during his visits to Bombay between 1917 and 1934 but this is the most logical time to continue to Mani Bhavan, the house become museum. It's not so far from the Towers of Silence but it will be easier to cab to 19, Laburnum Street, Gamdevi which is quietly residential.

Here, Gandhi learned to card and spin, met with colleagues and moulded the nation in his image. The house is a national monument and is a research institute. It includes a ground-floor library with more than 30,000 books for reference and lending on and by Gandhi and Gandhian thought. In the first floor auditorium, films are shown periodically and Gandhi's recorded speeches are played on request. The second floor room where he lived and worked has been preserved in its original setting and, adjoining is an exhibition of 28 tableaux depicting his life. There is also a photograhic gallery, some of his possessions and models of his birthplace and prison cell.

The museum is open every day from 9.30 a.m. to 6 p.m.

Bombay

Mahalaxmi Temple

As you continue down from Malabar Hill, north, as from the Towers of Silence, along the coast, you will pass Bombay's oldest temple, the Mahalaxmi Temple, appropriately for the city, dedicated to the goddess of wealth. There are effigies of several Hindu gods here.

Haji Ali's Mosque and Tomb

Now look out to sea where Haji Ali's mosque and tomb is accessible only at low tide so watch the time you spend here. Haji Ali was a Moslem saint who drowned on a pilgrimage to Mecca. The story goes that the casket containing his remains came to grief, floated and came to rest on a rock bed in the sea. His devotees built the mosque on the spot.

You can reach the mosque which is 500 yards out to sea via a causeway along which are many beggars waiting for generous pilgrims.

The plight of the beggars anywhere in India is distressing and Bombay has its large share of them. Some are professional beggars and can be quite insistent.

> **INFOTIP:** It is wise not to give to one beggar when there is a large concentration of them as those who have not received will expect to gain something too. Many work intersections at traffic lights and will even open car doors or place their hands through open windows. To avoid being bothered, keep the doors of taxi or chauffeur-driven vehicle locked. If it is hot and the car is not airconditioned, you will soon get into the habit of winding up the window when the vehicle comes to a stop. If you wish to help the poor, give to a recognized charity.

Mahalaxmi Racecourse

To the right of Haji Ali's tomb is the Mahalaxmi race course which Bombayites assert proudly is India's best and one of the finest in the East. The racing season extends from December to April on both days of each weekend. The course and the coastal road were built on land reclaimed from swamp.

Bombay

Light atop Mahalaxmi temple

Nehru Planetarium, Centre and Science Centre

A little further along off Dr. Annie Besant Road is the Nehru Planetarium which is situated in the same grounds as the Nehru Centre and Nehru Science Museum. At the planetarium, an image of the sky as seen from anywhere in the world at any time, past, present and future, 270,000 years either way, can be viewed. Shows in English are twice daily 3 and 6 p.m. daily except Mondays when the planetarium and also the Nehru Science Museum are closed.

The museum has a children's science park and a permanent gallery of exhibits relating to the properties of life. Other exhibits include an antique tramcar, railway engine, steam lorry and a more modern supersonic aeroplane.

Bombay

Worli Dairy

While in this neck of the woods, you can continue a bit further north to the Wurli Dairy if you are interested in seeing the pasteurizing, bottling and distribution of milk from 4 p.m. to 6 p.m. daily.

The road following the coast deviates from Dr Annie Besant to become Khan Abdul Gaffarkhan Marg off which the dairy is set. Now, how about an elephant or camel ride to brighten up your day?

Victoria Gardens and the Zoo

Retrace your way south east and get onto Dr E. Moses Road which passes the other side of the race course. You will come to an intersection of eight roads, known as **Saat Rasta** or **Jacob Circle**. Take K Khade Road till it joins N. M. Joshi Road. Cross the P.S. Mandik Bridge over the railway line and you will end up facing Victoria Gardens which are now also known as **Veer Mata Jijabai Bhonsle Udyan**. Entry is by Dr. Babasahbeb Arnbedkar Road. From the bridge, turn left and this street is the first to your right.

The nicely landscaped gardens covering 48 acres are open daily, except Wednesdays from 8 a.m. till 6 p.m. and, if riding a camel or elephant does not appeal, you could ride a pony from between 3 p.m. and 5 p.m. In the gardens established in 1863 is Bombay's zoo and the Victoria and Albert Museum.

The zoo houses a good selection of wild animals from zebras, lions, tigers and elephants to monkeys, deer and antelope. It also has rare birds among its feathered residents. The zoo is open in daylight hours, also closed Wednesdays along with the museum.

Victoria and Albert Museum

Now known as the **Dr Bhau Lad Museum**, the building is in the Italian Renaissance style. Its hours are 10.30 a.m. to 5 p.m., Thursdays from 10 a.m. to 4.45 p.m. and Sundays from 8.30 a.m. to 4.45 p.m. Entry is free except for Sundays.

The museum houses an interesting collection of archaeological finds from the city and State of Maharashtra, coins, metalware, weaponry and textiles and also photographs and maps tracing the history of Bombay. The big stone elephant which was brought from Elephanta Island in 1864 is set outside the building.

Bombay

Marvellous Markets

Get back on N.M. Josh Marg and direct a cabbie to take you to **Mahatma Jyotiba Phule Market**, formerly known as **Crawford Market** which is on Mata Ramabai Amredkar Road. You are now well back in the central district. Otherwise, get yourself back to Flora Fountain and walk to Crawford Market.

The market was established in 1867 and has high pitched roofs, a belfry with clock tower and is very much Bombay-Gothic in style. Inside, beneath huge glass-covered, iron ribbed halls, it is a fascinating place to stroll to see flowers, fruit, vegetables, fish, meat and cloth being sold, having arrived from several parts of India as well as being grown or produced in Maharashtra. There is where top city chefs and discerning housewives do their marketing and the haggling is marvellous to watch.

You'll need a guide in the know of the market to point out carvings made by the father of Rudyard Kipling who lived across the road.

Just across from Crawford Market is the **Sirrdl School of Art**, the building in which writer Rudyard Kipling, whose stories of India have delighted children and adults alike up till the present day, was born and lived the first years of his life. Visitors can enter to see Bombay art students at work.

This is an area of several markets and bazaars and, at the **Zaveri Bazaar**, you'll find a maze of streets where absolutely anything can be bought in about 3000 shops and stalls. One narrow lane will be dedicated to jewellery, another clothing, yet another cooking implements etc.

Laundry, Bombay style

Bombay

Painting wedding design on marble floor

Chor Bazaar in Central Bombay is also another must for the keen shopper, particularly for antiques, furniture intricately carved from rosewood, crystal, clocks, china and porcelain. It is perfect for the people-watcher and is also known as Bombay's thieves' market.

> **INFOTIP:** Watch your purse and wallet in the markets and bazaars. The crowds can be so crushing that it would be easy for you to be separated from your valuables by a light-fingered touch. But don't avoid these places. They are full of fabulous interest and many bargains if you bargain correctly. It's great sport.

The Chor Bazaar on Maulana Shaukatali Road, formerly Grant Road, behind **Bhendi Bazaar**, near Mohammed Ali Road is quite close to the **Radaut Tahera**. This is a marble mosque and mausoleum built by the *Dawoodi Bohra Moslems* in honour of their spiritual leader, the late *Dr. Syedna Taher Saifuddin*. The building has four silver doors, is lavishly decorated and the Koran inscribed on its inner walls in gold. The air conditioned **Fatemi mosque** has 17 arches representing the 17 Rakaat prayers.

Bombay

Fabulous Films

Seeing that Bombay is the world's movie-making capital, out-producing Hollywood with around 600 full-length films each year, it's an interesting outing to visit a studio to see one being made.

The film studios are hired by production companies for as long as they are needed so there's little point in turning up to a production company in the hope of catching some of the action. The stars and crews will be somewhere else filming. As earlier mentioned, The *Government of India Tourist Office* or the *Indian Tourist Development Corporation* (tel: 2023343) will, for a small charge, be able to arrange a visit to a set or studio where a so-called masala movie is being made. Masala, of course, is a mixture of Indian spices and an appropriate nickname for films which have almost every ingredient an escapist audience could desire.

For serious intellectual-type movies, you'll have to visit Calcutta to see them being produced and Madras for musical comedies and family-orientated films.

Naturally, there are movie theatres everywhere in Bombay. Some films are sub-titled in English and admission prices are very cheap. Watch the newspapers for titles and venues.

Outskirts

OUT FOR THE DAY

Panthers, Lions and Caves

About 42 kilometres north of Bombay is the **Krishnagiri Upvan** (or **Sanjay Gandhi**) national park in which are set the **Kanheri Caves**. These are worth seeing.

You can make your own way there by train to the Borivali Station then cab the 10 km extra distance to the caves. The alternative is to take an organized tour which includes the park and the caves or else hire a car with driver in Bombay. On Sundays, there is a bus service from the station to the Kanheri Caves but be warned buses will be very crowded as the excursion is popular with Bombayites.

A **Lion Safari Park** is by the national park entrance and you can take a 'safari' by closed four-wheel drive vehicle between 9 a.m. and 5 p.m. daily except Mondays. This is the only means by which you are permitted to enter the park. There's a small entry fee and each round trip takes about 30 minutes.

The entrance to the national park is a rather astounding former movie set resembling a fort. Within the park are **Lakes Powai**, **Vihar** and **Tulsi** but you won't see them if you are travelling direct to the caves on a somewhat rough and undulating road. You can take a mini train ride to the lakes. At **Powai** boats can be hired. The lakes supply Bombay with much of its water. There's also a crocodile park within the national park at Vihar Lake, home to several reptiles.

Juhu Beach, Bombay

Outskirts

As you approach the Kanheri Caves, you will see a sign which warns: *'Beware of Panthers. Do not linger in the park after 6.30 p.m.'* While the park closes at 5 p.m., visitors, particularly those who enjoy walking, have been known to miscalculate the time. The panthers come out of the bush to feed at dusk and they are not to be trifled with as the few villagers living within the park would attest.

There is another small charge to see the caves which should be approached slowly if the weather is hot as there are many steep steps and no chairs for hire as on Elephanta Island. There are soft drink stalls for refreshment on your return.

> **INFOTIP:** If you buy bottled soft drinks at any stall in India, you cannot take it with you but must drink it on the spot as vendors want the bottles for return. Not a bad idea in India is to carry a thermos flask if you intend doing a lot of walking. Buy the soft drink and pour the contents into the flask to keep cool.

The Kanheri Caves is one of the biggest monastic rock settlements in India. More than 100 caves were gouged out of rock by Buddhist monks in 1 BC and occupied for about 1000 years. The caves comprise vharas or small monastic chapels, a small university and include one of the largest standing Buddhas in India.

Earlier caves belonged to the Hinayana period of Buddhist architecture and many were excavated from an enormous, single circular rock. The Buddhist monks lived

Outskirts

in simple cells. The first second and third caves are most significant and interesting for their huge pillars, stupas and sculptures. Wear walking shoes for this excursion and plan on at least a half a day to complete it. Admission is free on Fridays. While you are in the vicinity, particularly if you have a chauffeured car, you might like to visit the **Jogeshwari Caves** which are also accessible from the Andheri station. Between Kanhari and Jogeshwari is the high-set **Aarey Milk Colony** which supplies Bombay with its milk. It is set in gardens, also able to be reached from Andheri station, and has good views. But possibly only those involved with the dairy industry would find it of particular interest. Admission is charged.

North of Borivali and across the **Uihas River**, which divides Bombay from the mainland on the road to Ahmedabad, is **Fort Bassein**. It is almost 80 km from Bombay by train to Bassein Road and a further 5 km by cab. Bassein was fortified by the Portugese from 1534 to the middle of the 18th century and a city of great majesty in which Portugese aristocracy lived. There were convents, churches and a cathedral.

Following the invasion by the local Marathas, the settlement was destroyed but some church and cathedral ruins remain. From Bassein Road station, the visitor can proceed almost 30 km by road (bus on Saturday afternoons, Sundays and public holidays) to **Vajreshwari Hot Springs**.

The Beaches of Bombay

Chowpatty Beach is out for swimming as earlier stated so if you can't get out of the central district and head north, be content with a hotel swimming pool.

About 20 km by train to Santacruz station near the domestic airport and then a short distance by road, taxi or public bus, is the 5km-long **Juhu beach**, closest to downtown Bombay. It is palm and hotel fringed by well-known international hotels such as Ramada and Holiday Inn and the Indian Centaur and smaller establishments. But here, too, it might be wiser to stick to hotel pools although you'll see a few Bombayites breasting the briny between October and May and can choose if you wish to join them.

But, particularly on weekends, the beach activity is fun -camel, donkey and pony rides, entertainers from acrobats to performing monkeys and there are sand-side stalls offering drinks and snacks.

Just back from the beach, the road heads north and the sea view is obscured by buildings, hotels and residences.

Goa

Here are several very casual restaurants and stalls. These are among the safest in Bombay to trust for an el cheapo meal on the run (provided you don't drink the water which looks so tempting, tinkling with ice cubes.)

Travel to Malad by train, about 40 km, to visit **Marve, Manori, Madh, Erangal** or **Aksa** beaches.

GO GO GO TO GOA

Just 25 minutes by airbus and 594 kilometres south from Bombay is Goa where beautiful beaches and a legacy of Portugese occupation from 1510 up till 1961 attract many domestic tourists and international visitors who have heard about this tiny State bordering Maharashtra. In May, 1987, Goa was separated from the Union Territory of Goa, Daman and Diu to become the 25th State in the Union of India.

One of the former Portuguese empire's richest and most strategically important conquests, Goa is still relatively unknown to Western visitors.

Beach, Goa

Goa

It is tropical and contrasts with bustling Bombay, a place to go to relax or, indeed, to experience not only Goa's distinctive cuisine, but the well-preserved relics of its colourful colonial past. It is a splendid State in which you can see alot in two to three days if you hire a tourist taxi or bus-it between major towns with the *Kalamba Tourist Corporation*, based in **Panaji**, the capital. The buses of Goa are better than those in most other Indian States, many being privately owned. Panaji, in some maps and literature, is spelled Panajim.

Motorbikes are for rent. You will see less but in greater detail if you hire a bicycle.

Goa covers an area of 3,702 square kilometres and is divided into 11 districts called talukas.

Several resort hotels offer three-night packages in the monsoon season when a day or so of rains is followed by one that is inevitably clear. Goa is fresh, clean and green during the monsoon season which is a time not to be dismissed by the visitor. The packages include airport transfers, accommodation, meals and use of all hotel facilities including sports. Hotels include the Hotel Oberoi, Bogmalo Beach,) Citade de Goa,(Dona Paula,) Majorda Beach Resort, Fort Aguada Beach Resort, Aguada (Beach) Hermitage and Taj Holiday Village. See further details under Hotels.

Goa is sandwiched between the hills on the **Western Ghats** and the **Arabian Sea**. It is verdant, undulating, brilliant with bougainvillea and has a 100-km coastline bordered by sandy beaches, palm and coconut trees.

It is possible to get to Goa by bus in about 15 and a half hours from Bombay. Check with the Government of India Tourist Office in Bombay on times (usually at night) and whether the coach is termed luxury or super luxury. Either are comfortable enough. But don't opt for a lesser standard.

> **INFOTIP:** When making your coach booking ascertain whether or not it has on-board videos. If so, prepare to be driven half-demented by continuous movie action in Hindi. Recently, the videos were banned on the Bombay-Goa route because foreign visitors objected to the noise. However, do check as the videos could be reinstated at any time.

Goa is connected from Bombay by train but the services are unreliable, slow and the trains are not renowned for their cleanliness. If you choose the train, travel first class. The most convenient station for Panaji is Margao from where you must take a taxi or bus to get to the capital. It

Goa

depends where you are staying on the north coast. Vasco da Gama may be a better choice.

There was an overnight ferry service from Bombay to Panaji for many years, conditions being somewhat spartan but the trip was interesting. It was discontinued but some tourist maps and literature still refer to the old service and shipping company. A new service was planned to be returned from November, 1989. Again, inquire of the GITO to establish if the service has resumed. If/when it does, it will not operate during the monsoon season.

While Goa does not yet have a marina, there are plans to establish one by the Citade de Goa resort hotel at **Vanguinim Beach, Dona Paula**, about 5 km from Panaji. This should be about the time the *National Water Sports Institute* is established in the early 1990s at the same spot. Visiting yachties entering the sheltered bay now are welcome to use the hotel complex's facilities (very Portugese and open in design) for a modest charge. The hotel has an excellent Portugese restaurant, dim and created at different levels to resemble a Portugese village in the evening. Sounds kitzch but it isn't. Here or in its more casual Goan/international semi open restaurant within sound of the sea, try the local feni -spirits made from cashew or coconut which you will find difficult to taste/buy outside Goa. They mix well with Limca, lemon-lime soft drink available everywhere.

Free berthing is also available to visiting yachtsmen at Dona Paula where the *Goa Yachting Association's* club house is situated further away from the Citade de Goa. Visitors are able to use club facilities.

Victoria Station at night

Goa Dourada - Golden Goa

Goa's pre-Christian chronicled history dates back to the third century BC and about 1600 years to follow of Hinduism. Goa then absorbed Jainism, Buddhism and (also resisted) Islam. The **Mandovi River**, on which Panaji is set, became a stopping-off point for great pilgrim galleons en route to Mecca.

In the Middle Ages, Goa was spice rich, part of the Arabian trade route and coveted by many nations. The Portugese, with the Cross, and led by Alfonso Albuquerque, turned up for their chop in 1510 after Vasco da Gama had paved the way to India. As ships full of wealthy cargoes, slaves, silk and stallions arrived in their thousands at this important trading centre, it developed in grand opulence, its churches as/or more resplendent than Rome's, its buildings and houses more gracious than in many parts of Europe and its fortresses daunting.

St Francis Xavier, a Jesuit, followed the Franciscan order to Goa but his impact is still most felt and acknowledged in this State where, now, all religious groups live in harmony, each with their own monuments and historic buildings, (at least those which were not destroyed by the Portuguese,) and each joyfully sharing the festvals and religious celebrations of the others.

Snake Charmer

Goa

Unless you are arriving by air on a charter or package, (in which case, your destination in Goa will be pre-planned,) you are well advised to head for Panaji (about 30 minutes by cab only, through very attractive countryside and villages.) The neat airport building is Portugese styled.

If you are arriving on an international flight, you'll need to go through customs and immigration. Goa's **Dabolim airport** is also connected with the Middle East (Dubai) and is a stop-off point for some Middle Eastern nationals.

The airport is actually almost equi-(short)-distant from the town of **Vasco da Gama** (30 km from Panaji) and **Bogmalo Beach** where the Oberoi Resort Hotel is set. The town named after Vasco da Gama, the Portugese explorer who actually died before ever reaching Goa, is neatly laid out with avenues and gardens. There is not a huge amount for visitors to experience here, apart from colourful fish and vegetable markets and pleasant streets but some travellers might find themselves in Vasco because of late arrival by air or train.

There is noteably good food at the Hotel Zuari and the Nanking Chinese Restaurant and no Vasco visitor should leave without taking a cab or bus up the steep winding road from town for a magnificent view of the Mormugao Harbour which is one of the best natural anchorages in India. It is a busy port for vessels exporting Goa's mining

Goa

products, fertilizers, tyres, electronic equipment, spices and other products. Occasionally, some passenger ships use the harbour as a port of call and there is plenty of local and traditional boating traffic to make the scene interesting.

Goa can be roughly divided into two, north and south. The south boasts silvery beaches while those of the north are a little brassier in colour but nonetheless satisfyingly sandy.

Set on the Mandovi River's southern bank, Panaji is a somewhat sleepy city with well-preserved buildings in the Portugese style. A climb to the top of **Altinho** (or hilltop) will reveal a panorama of river, red-roofed houses, gardens and avenues and the hill is probably the best place from which to orientate yourself to this pleasant place. You'll pass the **Patriachal Palace** and from the top will see a relatively new Indian temple.

Another way to get the feel of Panaji is to take an hour's cruise from the capital's wharf. Passengers are seated in chairs on top of the vessel and are entertained by a cultural song and dance show. You'll soon gain an impression of the Portugese influence in these enthusiastic performances. Drinks are available. The ship goes downstream some distance then returns upstream almost as far as the **Adil Shah Palace** which was occupied by Portugese Viceroys before the capital was shifted from Old Goa to Panaji in 1843. It is now the State's Secretariat. You pass the Hotel Mandovi which was once one of Goa's most elegant. It's still a good place to drop in for a drink and river view.

The evening cruise is best taken while it is still early as the waterfront lights tend to peter out away from the downtown area of the port and there is not much to see after dark although the continuous procession of ferries crossing the river and barges taking cargoes out to big ships at sea provide interest.

Walking around Panaji is the best way to experience the sense of it being a port town even though major activity has been transferred to Vasco da Gama. It has narrow, tavern-lined streets winding down to the river, avenues lined with gulmohar and acacia trees, shops set in pillared arcades, (which make shopping in the heat of day more pleasurable,) some stone buildings from 16th and 17th centuries and its Church of Our Lady of the Immaculate Conception is imposing.

The church is on a hill at one end of the **Municipal Gardens** in the heart of town. Masses held there are conducted in the native language, Konkani. One of Panaji's oldest buildings, it was founded before 1541, rebuilt in 1619 and is the focal point of the city's religious activities.

If you stand on the church steps looking down, you'll see that a *Government of India Tourist office* is located on the left hand side.(Communidada Building Church Square; telephone 3412.).But the tourism directorate is located in The Tourist Home which offers clean, economical dormitory accommodation. You'll find it by walking along the riverfront (upstream) crossing the bridge and taking the first turn right.

If you approach from the bus station, turn left before crossing the **Ourem creek**. When you cross the bridge, returning into town, you'll have a choice of three roads. Take the central one for the G.P.O. While in Panaji, also visit the monument to **Alfonso de Albuquerque**, who commanded the first Portugese to arrive in Goa in 1510. This is in the city's main square.

The tourist office can arrange for visitors to go inside some of the magnificent, privately-owned and beautifully maintained homes which, in charming gardens, reflect the distinctive Goan architecture with its Portugese influences. With their objets d'art, they are virtually musea in themselves. It is not possible to just wander in off the street. Allow as much time as possible for this interesting excursion to be organized.

Extensive use of passenger and car ferries is made in Goa and, even if you have hired a motorbike or bicycle, it is a pleasant way to break your mode of travel.

Sunday Mass, Goa

Marine Drive, Bombay

SOUTH GOA

Churches, Temples & Mosques

Here is a do-it-yourself tour of southern Goa, taking in as many of the highlights as possible in a short time after you have hired transport. Your alternative is to take a tour which includes many of the following attractions. You can buy an excellent road map from the tourist office. Most roads are very good but check in the monsoon season that no bridges are down.

About 30 minutes east and 10 km by bus is **Old Goa** or **Velha Goa**, which is the former capital. Before the arrival of the Portuguese, Old Goa was a busy, well-fortified city established by **Adil Shah** early in the 16th century as an alternative to his capital Bijipur but none of the pre-Portuguse buildings remain. However the legacy of the conquering Latins is rich indeed.

Old Goa has five main roads which converge in the central great square which is now dominated by a modern statue of Gandhi. The majority of buildings of real interest are within walking distance.

Heading west from **Mahatma Gandhi's** statue back towards Panaji, you'll see the most famous of Goa's churches, the **Basilica of the Born Jesus**. Built in the 16th century, it houses in an elaborate silver casket the well-preserved mortal remains of St. Francis Xavier, who first arrived in Goa in 1542. His subsequent journeys spreading Christianity took him to Indonesia, Japan, back to Goa and Malaysia (as it is now known) but he died off the coast of China on the final return to Goa.

First buried in Malacca, Malaysia, his body was returned to Goa where, after St Francis Xavier was canonized, he was placed at the Basilica. His body, (minus a few parts removed by relic hunters, some of his right hand, which was sent to Rome, and the hand's remains, despatched to the Jesuits of Japan,) is revealed to the public every tenth anniversary of his death, December 3, on which date, every year, Old Goa holds a festival in his name.

Next to the Basilica is the Professed House of the Jesuits, behind which is Our Lady of the Angels.

Opposite the Basilica is Goa's largest church, **Se Cathedral**, built in 1562 and dedicated to St Catherine. It has a marvellous vaulted interior and five bells, including the **Golden Bell**, Goa's biggest.

Next door is the **Archaeological Museum** and Portrait Gallery which contains Hindu sculptures and paintings of Goan governors. Adjacent is the **Church of St Francis of**

Charming offer of incense

Assisi. This is entered via a doorway which is the only existing example of Manueline architecture of the 15th century in Asia. Then comes the **Chapel of St Catherine**. Between the Basilica and the cathedral is the modern Statue of the **Cameos**.

North east of the cathedral is the **Arch of the Viceroys**, once an entrance into Adil Shah's Fort, which had been rebuilt by the Portugese as a gateway for governors arriving by boat into Goa. Just beyond is the baroque **Church of St Gaetjen**, now a place for newly ordained priests and known as the **Church of the Divine Providence**. Its style resembles Rome's St Peter's Basilica.

The ruins of the **Church of the Carmelites** and the chapel of Our Lady of the Mount are further east.

Return to Gandhi's central statue and head east towards Ponda for sight of the only remaining gate to St Paul's College and the chapel of **St Francis Xavier**.

Turning back towards Panaji, you will see the **Convent of St Monica**, fortress-like and opposite it, to the south, is the Church and Convent of **St John of God**. The tower of the **Church of St Augustine** is all that is left of the then, in 1602, biggest church in Goa. It is opposite the **Royal Chapel** of **St Anthony** which is little more than a stone's throw from **Our Lady of the Rosary** church, built in 1543.

In front of the Basilica of Born Jesus are souvenir and drink sellers if all this church-tramping works up a thirst.

Goa

Goa's carnival

> **INFOTIP:** If you arrive in Old Goa at a time of festival with thousands of others, locate the Missing Persons' Booth diagonally opposite the Basilica and agree to meet companions there should you become separated in the crowds.

A regular bus will take you on to the town of **Ponda** which is 30 km southwest of Panaji. Around Ponda are several significant temples and mosques, including **Safa Masjid**, the district's biggest and most famous mosque. It was built by Ibrahim Adil Shar of Bijapur in 1560. Its adjacent masonry tank where the pilgrims used wash has Maharab designs.

The **Shri Maguesh** temple on the northern outskirts of Ponda at the village of Priol is one of Goa's most spectacular temples with a magnificent white tower and chandeliered and pillared interior. It was built in the 16th century and dedicated to Lord Shiva.

Other temples of interest in the Ponda area include *Shri Gopal Ganapati* and *Shri Mahalaxmi* containing a rare gallery of wooden images of Vishnu and Shri Nagesh, also dedicated to Shiva.

Driving south from Ponda, you can cross the River Zuari at Borlm and proceed down to Margao, a bustling, major town with a daily market and lots of Goan atmosphere. It is a great place to wander, has its share of gardens, old mansions and villas and its **Church** of the **Holy Spirit**, built in 1564 and re-built in 1675, is worth visiting. It is also just a short distance (accessible by public bus) from Colva Beach. This is one of Goa's safest beaches, is popular with local fisherfolk, and has clean budget accommodation in Government Tourist Cottages along with good choices of other hotels. From Panaji, the bus ride to Colva takes about an hour.

Trains and Waterfalls

It is from Margao that you can take a train through forest, jungle and farmland right across to the eastern periphery of Goa. It is a long journey to reach the **Dudhsagar Waterfall** and many visitors go by train from Colem for an hour or else travel by forest road during the dry months.

Frankly, the falls are not so interesting during the dry season but are a must for monsoon-season visitors. The **Candepar River** cascades hundreds of metres into a big gorge to become one of Goa's most spectacular natural features. Legend has it that a princess bathing in the river noticed a roaming prince and was at the mercy of his roving eyes. She incanted her deity to protect her modesty. Her request was fulfilled by a shroud of mist which later, tumbled downwards as milk - which it still does today.

The falls become the lifeline to the ecosystem of the **Bhagwan Mahavir Wildlife Sanctuary** which is popular with trekkers and wildflower enthusiasts. But it is recommended that trekkers seek the guidance of a ranger through the Goa Tourism Development Corporation which conducts special rail tours to the falls in conjunction with the South Central Railway as there are also wild animals in the sanctuary. The corporation's travel division is located at Trionara Apartments, near Cine El Dorado, Panaji. (tel: 6515, 4132.) Accommodation in the area can also be arranged.

Now, back in Margao, you can travel south through attractive landscape to Chaudi before turning towards the beautiful, unspoiled and relatively unknown **Palolem Beach** then the similar, palm-fringed Agonda. Here, the huge, luxurious Hotel Sima complex with 18-hole golf

Goa

course, lawn tennis and huge gardens will delight visitors when it opens.

More directly accessible from Margao are a greater concentration of beaches with accommodation, starting from Cavelossim Beach then proceeding north towards Panaji. Near Cavelossim are beaches with accommodation, starting from Cavelossim Beach then proceeding north towards Panaji. Near Cavelossim is the new The Old Anchor Resort delightfully set on an isthmus between the River Sul and the sea. You won't find it on a map but head for the beach and you'll see it. It offers apartment accommodation and you can self-cater or eat at the restaurant.

Lovely **Fatrade Beach**, just north, is the location for the newly-opened Ramada Hotel Resort and you'll find **Varka** and **Benavli Beaches** then **Colva** before **Majorda Beach** with its popular, well-established resort. This property is 20 acres of lush gardens, 20 minutes from *Dobulim Airport* or 10 from *Margao*. It has both indoor and outdoor pools, a super stretch of beach and offers riding as a sport.

Just north west is **Bogmalo Beach** where the Oberoi Bogmalo Hotel has all rooms sea-facing, a health club and water sports facilities. It is right on the beach. If you have not tasted the local feni, (coconut or cashew liquor,)ask for it here in the cool breezeway bar/lounge area as a cocktail with pineapple juice and other secret ingredients. It is terrific. Now, without too many under your belt, you are almost back in Panaji.

The **Dona Paula Beach** section occupied by the Citade de Goa is private for guests and the best beach around Panaji, clean, with water sports and visitors are not bothered by local vendors when sunbaking - as sometimes happens on public beaches.

At Dona Paula itself, there is a fishing village and pleasure boats are available for hire.

On a bluff overlooking Dona Paula is an interesting viewpoint which looks a little like a Greek temple. It is a spot to which local tourists flock to hear the story of the young Indian girl who fell in love with a Portugese. Her parents did not sanction the match so she suicided from this point to the rocks below. Grief-stricken, he followed her. Their statues are atop and you can climb steps to meet them.

By the bridge, there are souvenir stalls manned by smiling Goans who are friendly and jesting even if one does not wish to buy, the qualities of friendliness and helpfulness being inherent in most of the people.

From the bridge, you can take a ferry to cross the wide **Mormugao Bay** to **Vasco da Gama** in about 30 minutes, a nice excursion which could occupy half a day or provide a different way to get back to the airport via Vasco. You can

Goa

The movie capital

also ferry back from Dona Paula to Panaji wharf which is about 7 km by bus.

Wide-sanded **Mirimar Beach** is closest to downtown Panaji but while the locals brave the undertow, it is probably too polluted for most westerners.

Niceties of the North

To explore the north, drive from Panaji along the **Mandovi River** road west in the direction of Old Goa until you reach Ribandar. Here, a queue of vehicles will indicate where the car ferry leaves. The road at the northern side leads up Chorao Island about 35 km to Narve village and the **Shri Saptakoteshwar Temple**. The original temple was situated in **Diwadi Island** and its idol brought to this site. In about 1668, **Chatrapati Shiravji**, in a campaign against the Portugese, ordered the temple's renovation to house a multi-faceted lingum.

Continue to **Maem**, a green lake with pleasure and fishing boats, bordered by another group of basic Government Tourist Cottages. Take a loop through the town of **Bicholim** heading roughly south west to **Mapusa** which is at the cross roads of the network of highways in north Goa. The Portugese influence here is strong in its buildings but its weekly fair on Fridays is its major attraction, particularly if you are in self-contained accommodation at nearby beaches and need a good variety of supplies for your stay.

Goa

Choice of Fish, Bogmalo, Goa

From here, it's an easy run to **Vagator Beach** through a picturesque fishing village. The road now continues south from which you can deviate into some of Goa's most marvellous beaches - **Anjuna**, where the hippie element has been largely eliminated, Baga, where there is reasonable sea anchorage for yachties and **Calangute** which the brochures describe as the Queen of Beaches. It's nice in a touristy way but some visitors would dispute the accolade.

Next south are **Candolim** and **Sinquerim** beaches before you reach **Fort Aguada** where the Taj has a very upmarket resort Fort Aguada from which the coastline previously mentioned extends like a vast sunworshipper's paradise.

Guests/delegates at a former British Commonwealth Heads of Government Meeting (CHOGM) were transported through groves bordered by bougainvillea to lovely hilltop villas by buggy for magnificent coastal views and luxury accommodation which is now experienced by affluent visitors. The fort, after which the hotel is named,

Goa

is probably Goa's most impressive. Once a water-stop-off place for passing ships returning to Portugal and built in 1612, its prison interned German prisoners during the last world war. Its beacon is visible for a long distance out to sea. The lighthouse was the first lit in Asia in 1864.

The much-less expensive Taj Holiday Village below the Fort Aguada Resort Taj is equally accessible to the fort and also shares the same marvellous stretch of beach.

Retrace your way north as far as Calangute then head south east to the village of **Belim** where you'll meet the flat-bottomed ferry which will return you across the Mandovi River to Panaji.

There are many more excursions to be taken into this rich, cultured Indian State but the above should give insight into Goa to those who have just two to three days to spend. This does not include much lazing on lovely beaches or beside crystal clear pools. This has been go go go in Goa. But even at such a pace, it will be an experience that will inspire you to return to re-discover Golden Goa at a slower speed.

Outskirts

CAVING IN TO INDIA

Ellora and Ajanta

The depth of fascination and variety of Goa's many attractions may seem too much to contemplate if one has only a couple of days to spend side-tripping out of Bombay. A shorter alternative or, ideally, an addendum to Goa is to travel by air, bus or train almost directly east of Bombay to **Aurangabad**, just over 390 km. It is 30 minutes away by air and about nine hours by train. *Indian Airlines* has daily flights and Vayudoot thrice weekly flights from Bombay.

Aurangabad is the jumping off point to the famous **Ellora** and **Ajanta Caves** with their amazing rock-cut temples, respectively 30 and 100 km from the town named after the last of the six great Moghul emperors, Aurangzeb, son of Shahajahan who commissioned the Taj Mahal.

The uncrowded town is remarkable in itself, mostly for its near replica of the Taj Mahal. The **Bibi-ka-Maqbara** was built by Aurangzeb, the son who had imprisoned his father and sought to copy the Taj Mahal as a monument to his own dead wife, **Dilras Banu Begum**. If you haven't time to see the Taj, this monument will be of interest though nowhere near as spectacular. However, even if you have been awed by the marble ediface in Agra, you will still recognize the special charm of the Aurangabad tomb and be entranced by the legends which surround it and the town.

From the railway station in the south of town, make your way north along Station Road to the tourist office for information and accommodation if you have not pre-booked. If you arrive early in the day by whatever means, you need only one night's stay. The cheaper hotels and eateries are located in the south. The *Maharashtra State Road Transport Corporation* has city bus services from the railway station to major points in town.

The central bus station is in the centre of town on Dr Ambedker Road which is really a northern extension of Station Road. On the road which criss-crosses, and leads to Ellora and about 3 km north of the station, is the government Aurangabad Ashok Hotel on Dr Ragenda Prasad Road. It's next to the **Indian Airlines** office, is centrally located and approved tourist taxis and coaches can be hired here. Also tours of the area can be booked.

There are many hotels in this old district. The two international hotels, the Ajanta Ambassador and the

Outskirts

Welcomegroup Rama are close together out of town on the airport road.

To get to the **Bibi-ka-Maqbara**, travel north from the central bus station. Don't cross the river but continue until you reach Ghati Road. This curves further north to become the road to the Aurangabad Caves which are about 5 km from town. But before, a right hand fork leads to the mausoleum of Aurangzeb's wife. Believed to have been built between 1657 and 1661, it is reputed to be the best example of Moghul architecture on the Deccan plateau. The mausoleum is set in a square, walled area of 137,000 square metres.

Return to the main road and continue the extra 2 km to the Aurangabad Caves which, while they pale against the awesome Ellora and Ajanta Caves, are worth seeing for their beautiful sculptures, particularly in the seventh cave. They have been excavated in three groups on a small hill and comprise 12 Buddhist caves in all. They are believed to date from between the third and 11th centuries. The western group features monasteries or viharas. In the eastern group is a large Buddha and the seventh cave has intrictately sculptured female figures wearing little but jewellery.

These caves are open from sunrise to sunset and can be reached from the Bibi-ka-Maqbara and town by auto-rickshaw.

Daulatabad Fort

It's an idea to turn back into town then west for 30 km and the Ellora Caves on the same day if you are short of time. On the way to Ellora, and about 13 km from Aurangabad, you will see the impressive **Daulatabad Fort**, (meaning city of fortunes,) built by Bhila, Raja of the Yadava dynnasty in 1187. It rates as one of the most impregnable and venerable forts in India. Originally called **Deogiri**, it was renamed by Emperor Mohammad-bin-Tughlaq when he established his capital there in around 1326. This move involved marching the people of Delhi the gruelling 1100 km from the capital. Many did not survive.

The fortification has a moat, a spiral passage, carved from solid rock and multiple doorways. There is a mosque which was a former Jain temple, also a Mohgul palace where the last king of Golconda was held prisoner for several years before his death. The Chand Minar is an inspiring 60-metre tower. A climbing exploration of the fort is fascinating and rewarding for its hilltop views.

Outskirts

Ellora Caves

The Kailasa Temple is a mammoth free-standing shrine about twice the area of Greece's Parthenon and one and a half times as high at 50 by 33 metres and 30 metres high. There is a small gopuram at the entrance and huge pillars at either side. These depict Shiva, Parvati and Gajalakshmi above Ravana, the demon king, shaking **Mount Kailash** the mythical Himalayan mountain after which the temple was named and the abode of Lord Shiva.

The temple, the most spectacular feature at the Ellora site, was chiselled from an enormous single rock by hand into gateway, pavillions, vestibule, assembly hall, inner sanctum and tower.

Of the 34 caves gouged out of rock at Ellora, 12 are Buddhist which are essentially quite simple and most are monasteries and include large Buddhas. They date for about 200 years from around 600 AD while the 17 Hindu temple caves are believed to have been commenced at about 900 AD. The Kailasa, of course, is the masterpiece of determination and artistry but others are marvellously elaborate. The builders gouged downwards, eliminating the need for scaffolding, being possessed with great knowledge of rock formation. Five Jain caves, finished in about 1000AD, are smaller than the Buddhist and Hindu caves but they contain some fine, intricate sculptures.

From Aurangabad, it is 106 km north to the **Ajanta Caves**, (there is a bus service) so a day should be scheduled for a return visit unless you wish to stay in fairly modest accommodation at **Fardapur** which is about 5 km from the caves and has access by regular bus services. If you wish to view both Ellora and Ajanta Caves chronologically, go to Ajanta first.

Ajanta is comprised of 30 caves hewn from rock, comprising either chapels (chaityas) or monasteries (viharas.) The caves were created between 200 BC and 600 AD yet, despite the long period, they maintain a continuity of concept. While excavated to allow natural light to illuminate them at certain times of day, some may be dim or dark at the time of your visit.

INFOTIP: As at Elephanta Island off Bombay and Ellora, take a torch with you so you do not miss the detail of sculptures in the former caves and the outer sculptures and inner paintings of the Ajanta Caves. If you forget your torch, a charge is made to show the light to groups of 20 people. One buys a lighting ticket.

Outskirts

The Ajanta paintings reflect the life of Buddha and his experiences on earth before enlightenment. Some of the most exciting and exquisite works belong to the large areas devoted to Buddha's early earthly life when he was surrounded by beautiful women and succumbing to the luxury of court life.

The paintings reflect the change of Buddhist artistic thought from severe austerity to creativity which embraced a sensuousness more in keeping with the Hindu style of expression. Most of the frescoes and sculptures are remarkably well preserved because the remoteness of the site defied vandalizing conquerors.

There is an entry fee (except Friday which is free) and the caves are open from 9 a.m. to 5.30 p.m.

State Transport offers an Ellora and City Tour daily and an Ajanta Caves excursion daily, starting 30 minutes before the nominated time from the bus stand at the railway station. Maharashtra Tourist Development Corporation at the Holiday Resort (tel 4713) on Station Road, just up from the station, also runs tours as does, subject to booking, ITDC. For details, contact Ashok Travel and Tours at the Hotel Aurangabad Ashok. Tel: 4143.

Caving in India

PART III
Accommodation

Nariman Point, aerial view

HOTELS

General Notes

The third section of this Info-Guide is an up-to-date list of hotels in Bombay, its suburbs and Goa in descending order of excellence from five star deluxe, through five, four, three, two to one star. These are with the exception of some in Goa which have not yet received a star rating but which have been inspected by one author and rate from between two star and five-star deluxe. The hotels are listed as Bombay and Suburbs and Goa.

There are no camping facilities in Bombay or Goa.

The criteria for classification has been set by India's Department of Tourism and is based on all facilities of each, individual establishment from the size of the room to the qualifications of hotel personnel. Most of the hotels listed have been government approved. But where, only in Goa, in the very latter section, they have not, does not mean that they are disapproved of. Gaining star-rating is a long and involved process in India, involving many inspections and time in which the hotels must fulfill the standards required to meet the star- rating sought. A Goan facility which has accommodated British Commonwealth heads of State has, to date, not been star- classified. But there is no question that it has not been approved by its guests and what it is.

Star-ratings do not indicate that all prices in one category are the same. They can vary. Also each vary in the type of additional taxes charges. The taxes can include government, sales, luxury, service and taxes on food and liquor. Where there is a service charge, tipping is not expected. Business travellers will also see at a glance the facilities available.

If air conditioning is available, it will be listed.

Some hotels have listed under their facilities Bar Permit or Permit Room. This means that to be able to order alcohol other than beer, visitors must produce their permit to do so in areas where there is partial prohibition. See the Restaurant/ Food section of this book for details on gaining the permit.

When they are good, Indian hotels are very very good, superior in the world. In most accommodations, accounts must be paid in foreign currency - cash, travellers' cheques or by credit card. Inquire about the method of payment expected in hotels which do not list credit card facilities when booking or checking in.

Special rates are usually applicable in the monsoon

Accommodation

season and/or for groups. Goa has special monsoon packages.

The Indian Tourist Development Corporation operates a chain of hotels under the name Ashok. From two to five star, these are inevitably reliable. Inquire of the Government of India Tourist Office in your home country about special discount rates applicable if your Indian sojourn will be in Ashok hotels, with the exception of Bombay which does not yet have an Ashok hotel.

Checkout times vary from 10 a.m. to noon. Some hotels, if not fully pre-booked, will offer special day room rates to late-departing travellers.

When booking, inquire on which plan the room rate is structured. The American Plan includes room and three meals. Modified American Plan is room, breakfast, lunch or dinner. The European Plan is room only.

Where car rental is listed as a facility, this is rental with driver.

LEGEND

- R - Restaurants/dining rooms
- C - Conference Rooms
- B - Bars
- SP - Swimming Pool
- TV - Television/Video
- RM - Room Service
- T - Tennis Court
- G - Golf Course
- AC - Air-Condition
- BC - Business Centre
- D - Discotheque
- CC - Credit Cards
- SS - Secretarial Services
- CR - Car Rental
- BP - Bar Permit

BOMBAY

The Oberoi
Nariman Point
Bombay 400021
Tel. 202 5757
AC, TV, RM, R, SP, CC, BC

The Leela Penta
Kempinski
Bombay 400 059
Tel. 636 3636
R, AC, C, SP, TV, RM, B, BC, CC

Accommodation

The Oberoi Towers
Nariman Point
Bombay 400 021
Tel. 202 4343
R, AC, SP, D, T, SS, TV, BC, CC

Hotel President
90 Cuffe Parade
Colaba
Bombay 400 005
Tel. 495 0808
R, AC, RM, SP, SS, BC, CR

Taj Mahal Intercontinental
Apollo Bunder
Bombay 400039
Tel. 202 3366
Fax. (022) 287 2711
R, AC, RM, SP, CC

Centaur Hotel
Bombay Airport
Bombay 400 099
Tel. 612 6660
R, AC, C, B, RM, SS, TV, SP, T, G, CC

Hotel Airport Kohinoor
J.B. Nagar
Andheri-Kurla Road
Andheri (E)
Bombay 400 059
Tel. 634 8548/49, 634 4334, 63 4566
R, AC, C, CC

Ramada Inn Palm Grove
Juhu Beach
Juhu
Bombay 400 049
Tel. 614 9361, 614 9343
Fax. 9122-614 2105
R, AC, C, B, R, SP, TV, SS, BP, CC

The Resort
11 Madh Marve Road
Aksa Beach
Malad (W)
Bombay 400 095
Tel. 682 3331
R, RM, SP, T, TV, SS, C, CC

Sun-n-Sand Hotel
39 Juhu Beach
Bombay 400 049
Tel. 620 1811
R, AC, C, SP, TV, BP, CC

Holiday Inn
Balraj Sahani Marg
Juhu
Bombay 400 049
Tel. 620 4444
R, AC, RM, TV, SP, T, CC

Fariyas Hotel
25 Off Arthur Bunder Road
Colaba
Bombay 400 005
Tel. 204 2911
R, AC, TV, CC

Hotel Nataraj
135 Netaji Subhash Road
Bombay 400 020
Tel. 204 4161
R, AC, TV, SS, C, CR, CC

Hotel Tunga International
M.I.D.C
Off Mahakali Cave Road
Andheri (E)
Bombay 400 093
Tel. 636 6010, 634 6666
R, AC, C, RM, CR, BP, CC

Hotel Apollo
22 Lansdowne Road
Apollo Bunder
Colaba
Bombay 400 039
Tel. 202 0223
R, AC, C, TV, BP, CR, CC

Hotel Hilltop International
43 Pochkanwala Road
Worli
Sea-Face
Bombay 400 025
Tel. 493 0860
R, AC, CC

Accommodation

Hotel Oberoi Towers

Ascot Hotel
38 Garden Road
Colaba Causeway
Bombay 400 039
Tel. 24 0020
R, AC, TV, CR

Hotel Atlantic
18-B Juhu Tara Road
Bombay 400 049
Tel. 612 2440-1, 612 6716
R, AC, C, BP, CR

Hotel Bombay International
29 Marine Drive
Bombay 400 020
Tel. 202 6060
R, AC, C, D, BP

Citizen Hotel
960 Juhu Beach
Juhu Tara Road
Bombay 49
Tel. 612 3790, 612 3793, 612 3159
R, AC, TV, C, BP, CR, CC

Ritz Hotel
5 Jamshedji Tata Road
Churchgate
Bombay 20
Tel. 22 0141, 22 0116
R, AC, B, RM, C, TV, CC

Hotel Sands
39/2 Juhu Beach
Bombay 400 049
Tel. 57 1451, 57 1543
R, AC, TV, SS, B

Hotel Kemps Corner
131 August Kranti Marg
Bombay 400 036
Tel. 822 4646, 811 8996
AC, TV, CC

Hotel King's
5 Juhu Tara Road
Juhu
Bombay 400 049
Tel. 614 8449-50-52
R, AC, TV, BP, CC

Accommodation

Hotel Rosewood
99/C Tulsiwadi
Tardeo
Bombay 400 034
Tel. 494 0320-29
AC, C, R, TV, BP, CR

Hotel Samraaj
Chakala Road
Andheri (East)
Bombay 400 099
Tel. 634 9311-15
R, AC, B, RM, CC

Sea Green Hotel
145 Marine Drive
Bombay 400 020
Tel. 22 2294, 22 2386, 22 2364
AC, TV, CC

Sea Palace Hotel
26 P.J. Ramchandani Marg
Bombay 400 039
Tel. 24 1828
R, C, AC, CR

Hotel Galaxy
Prabhat Colony
Santacruz (East)
Bombay 400 055
Tel. 612 5223, 614 4980
R, AC, CC

Hotel Park Lane
95 Dadasaheb Phalke Road
Dadar
Bombay 400 014
Tel. 44 8241-5
R, AC, C, CR

Sea Side Hotel
39/2 Juhu Beach
Bombay 400 049
Tel. 620 0293/297
R, AC, SP, CC

Hotel Ajanta
8 Juhu Road
Bombay 400 049
Tel. 612 4890-91
R, AC, TV, RM, SS, BP, CC

Accommodation

Hotel Jal
Nehru Road
Vile Parle (East)
Bombay 400 057
Tel. 612 3820
R, RM, TV, C, BP, CC

Shalimar Hotel
August Kranti Marg
Bombay 400 036
Tel. 822 1311
R, AC, RM, TV, BP, CC

Hotel Transit
Near Bombay Airport
Off Nehru Road
Vile Parle (East)
Bombay 400 099
Tel. 612 9325/6, 612 1087, 612 0661
R, AC, TV, BP, CC

West End Hotel
45 New Marine Lines
Bombay 400 020
Tel. 29 9121
R, AC, C, B, RM, TV, CC

Astoria Hotel
4 J.T. Road Churchgate
Bombay 400 020
Tel. 22 1514
R, AC, BP, CR

Hotel Caesars Palace
313 Linking Road
Khar
Bombay 400 052
Tel. 54 2311-3
R, AC, BP

Hotel Mayura
352 Linking Road
Bombay 400 052
Tel. 649 4416-19-21-23-24
AC, R, RM, TV, B, BP, CC

Hotel Parkway
Ranade Road
Shivaji Park
Sea-Face Dadar
Bombay 400 028
Tel. 45 3361-62-63
R, AC, B, BP

Hotel Godwin
41 Garden Road
Bombay 400 039
Tel. 24 1226, 287 2050
R, AC, TV, RM, BP, CC

Grand Hotel
17 Sprott Road
Bombay 400 038
Tel. 26 8211
R, AC, B, RM, CC

Accommodation

Hotel Diplomat
24/26 B.K. Boman Behram Marg
Colaba
Bombay 400 039
Tel. 202 1661
R, AC, B, C, TV, CC

Hotel Airport Plaza
70-C Nehru Road
Vile Parle (E)
Bombay 400 099
Tel. 612 2979, 612 3390-93, 612 9429
R, AC, SS, B, D, SP, TV, CC

The Ambassador Hotel
Chruchgate Extn
Veer Nariman Road
Bombay 20
Tel. 204 1131
R, AC, C, B, RM, TV, CR, CC

Hotel Rajdoot
19 Jackeria Bunder Road
Cotton Garden
Bombay 400 033
Tel. 851 4444
R, AC, C, TV, BP, CR

Garden Hotel
42 Garden Road
Colaba
Bombay 400 039
Tel. 24 1476, 24 1700
R, AC, TV

Hotel Heritage
Sant Savta Marg
Byculla
Bombay 400027
Tel. 851 4891-5
R, AC, C, TV, BP, CC

Accommodation

Fun during Holiday Festival

GOA HOTELS

Hotel Chalston
Cobro Vad'do
Calangute
Bardez
Goa
Tel. 80
R, AC, CR

The Taj Holiday Village
Sinquerim
Bardez
Goa 403 515
Tel. 7514-17
AC, C, R, SP, CR, T, SS

Aguada Hermitage
Sinquerim
Bardez
Goa 403 515
Tel. 7501-07
R, AC, SP, T, C

The Old Anchor
Cavelossim Beach
Salcete
Margoa
Goa
Tel. 20729
R, AC, SP, T, G, CC

The Fort Aguada Beach Resort
Sinqurim
Bardez
Goa 403515
Tel. 7501-07
R, AC, SP, T, TV

Hotel Airport
Airport Road
Chicalim
Vasco da Gama
Tel. 2165, 2615
AC, R, RM, B

Accommodation

Oberoi Bogmalo Beach
Bogmalo
Goa 403 806
Tel. 2191, 3311-15
R, AC, SP, TV, CC

Hotel Fidalgo
18th June Road
Panjim-Goa 403001
Tel. 6291, 99, 6267, 3330-32
R, AC, RM, B, SP, TV, C, SS, CR, CC

Keni's Hotel
18th June Road
Panjim
Goa 403 001
Tel. 4581-83
R, AC, C, TV, CC

Hotel Mandovi
D.B. Bandodkar Marg
Panaji
Goa
Tel. 6270-79
R, AC, TV, C, CR, CC

Hotel Baia Do Sol
Baga Beach
Calangute
Goa
Tel. 84/85
R, AC, CR, CC

Hotel Golden Goa
Dr. Atmaram Borkar Road
Panaji-Goa-403 001
Tel. 6231-6239
R, AC, TV, RM, SP, CC

Hotel La Paz Gardens
Swatantra Path
Vasco-da-Gama
Goa 403802
Tel. 2121, 2738, 3302
R, AC, TV, SS, CC

Hotel Metropole
Margoa-Goa (INDIA)
Tel. 21516, 21169
R, AC, C, SP, CC

Hotel Diamond
Vagator Beach
Post Anjuna
Bardez
AC, R, SP, C, B

Calangute Beach Resort
Umta-Vaddo Calangute
Goa 403 516
Tel. 63
R, B

Cidade De Goa
Vainguinim Beach
Dona Paula
Goa 403 004
Tel. 3301, 3307
R, AC, C, B, TV, SP, T, CC

Majorda Beach Resort
Majorda
Salcette
Goa 403 713
Tel. 20751/52, 20203/04
R, AC, C, B, SP, T, CC

Noah's Ark
Bamboo Motels & Hotels
Verem Reis Magos
Goa
Tel. 7321, 7322, 7323, 7324
R, AC, SP, T

Hotel Nova Goa
Dr. Atmaram Borkar Road
Panaji-Goa 403 001
Tel. 6231-6239
R, AC, TV, RM, SP, CC

Hotel Silver Sands
Colva Beach
Colva 403 708
Salcette Goa
Tel. 21645, 21646
R, AC, SP, B, CC, CR

Ramada Beach Resort
Fatrade Beach
Goa
AC, SP, G, T, R, C, CC

PART IV
Practical Information

PRACTICAL INFORMATION

A-Z Summary

ADVANCE PLANNING	119
CINEMAS	128
CRIME	146
DANCE	129
DOCTORS	see Help
ELECTRICITY	125
ENTRY REGULATIONS	122
Customs	122
Duty Free Imports	123
Currency	123
ENTERTAINMENT	125
Art Galleries and Museums	125
Goa Museums and Art Galleries	127
Children's Entertainment	127
EXHIBITIONS	129
EMERGENCIES	see Help
FESTIVALS	130
GETTING TO INDIA	124
GETTING AROUND BOMBAY	137
HELP	142
Consulates	142
Medical Emergencies	144
Police Emergencies	145
Death	145
Lost Property	146
Replacement of Certain Items	146
LIBRARIES WITH BOOKS IN ENGLISH	148
METRIC SYSTEM	180
MONEY	see Business Guide
MOTORING	147
Rental Vehicles with Driver	147
POST OFFICES	149
PUBLICATIONS IN ENGLISH	148
English Language Booksellers	148
RADIO/TELEVISION	134
RELIGIOUS SERVICES IN ENGLISH	150
RESTAURANTS AND NIGHT LIFE	151
SEMINARS	133
SHOPPING	166
SPORTS AND ATHLETICS	170
TELEPHONE AND TELEGRAPH	172

THEATRE AND MUSIC	134
TIME	174
TIPPING	174
TOURIST SERVICES	174
TOURS	177

Advance Planning

The Government of India Tourist Office, the Tourist Development Corporation and Air India has offices in many parts of the world to help you plan your itinerary or stopover.

What to bring

Documents

All visitors to India need a current passport and visa. Three types of visa are issued - tourist, non- tourist and entry. It depends on the purpose of the visit. Tourist visas for 90 days may be extended by applying to Foreigners Regional Registration offices in Bombay, Delhi, Madras or Calcutta or at district headquarters of Superintendent of Police. In Bombay, the Foreigners Regional Registration Office is by Mahatma Phule Market. Tel: 4150446.

People in transit to other parts of the world must produce onward tickets in order to gain a transit visa of 15 days to be used within three months of the issuing date. A double-way transit visa allows the visitor two trips through India for a maximum of 15 days each time.

First issued for 90 days to people intending professional or business dealings in India, an entry visa can be extended for a further 90 days. If a trip could exceed extensions of six months, application must be made two months in advance to an Indian Embassy or Mission out of India.

Visa issuing fees are charged by embassies abroad to foreigners with the exception of nationals from Afghanistan, Czechoslovakia, Denmark, Greece, Hungary, Iran, Norway, Poland, Rumania, Russia, San Marino, Sweden, Uraguay and Yugoslavia.

Also bring credit cards and a driver's licence, preferably an international licence which may be needed for motor cycle rental especially in Goa.

Americans will need receipts of purchases for their own customs. All foreigners should check with their own customs departments on current legislation on the importation home of ivory.

Clothing

India is so vast that its climatic conditions vary greatly but for Bombay and Goa bring the lightest of cotton garments between February and May when in Bombay,

Practical Information

temperatures are likely to reach the high 30s. Also in Goa at the same time, humidity can be high. In June, the monsoon season arrives and most rain falls between then and September. Bring some light wool garments. But it doesn't rain all the time. Storms can be followed by sunny periods. In Goa, the monsoon season can be a good time to visit. Most of Bombay and Goa are pleasantly sunny during India's winter, November to February. You can buy suitable clothing very cheaply in India.

The Indian people dress modestly so bear this in mind when dressing for the street and excursions which may include places of religious worship. Brief shorts and tops will offend. Men can wear shorts but women should not. Men should not go bare chested. Some top class hotels may require neat, casual dress in restaurants.

Pack a swimming costume. Nude and topless bathing is not permitted.

Odds and Ends

A towel for swimming. Top hotels with pools provide them to guests (some free, others for a small fee,) but more modest establishments do not. Also bring a face towel to remain moist in a plastic bag to refresh yourself if driving in non-airconditioned vehicles. Pack a portable clothes line, health (see below) and personal necessities such as spectacles, contact lenses and sun cream. Women should bring their preferred brands of cosmetics, toiletries and tampons as they may be unavailable. Bring tissues to act as toilet paper in emergencies. Padlock your suitcase and bring another with you for your door if you are staying in accommodations which may have inadequate security.

While films and camera batteries are available in the cities and larger towns, don't run the risk of running out and bring extra.

> **INFOTIP:** Passengers flying in on Air India and flying internally are not permitted to include some types of batteries, such as those powering certain cameras, in their hand luggage. Pack them (and maybe the appliance well- wrapped in clothing) in luggage to be stowed in the cargo as buying batteries at your destination will represent inconvenience and may not be immediately available.

Medical Tips

Take out adequate health cover in your travel insurance. Should you become ill, you will need it against private

Practical Information

hospital care or the attentions of a hotel's doctor whose charges may be high. Naturally, keep all receipts for fees charged to present on your return. If you intend arriving via a yellow fever infected country, ensure you are vaccinated before leaving home. This is India's only vaccination requirement.

However, because you may travel in areas where sanitation is poor, it is strongly recommended that you consult your doctor before leaving and consider having cholera, combined tetatus/typhoid, and gamma globulin (against hepatitus A,) innoculations. If you are a frequent traveller to eastern countries, also consider protection against hepatitus B.

If you are travelling in both northern and southern India, tell your doctor. Two different tablets to protect you against two strains of malaria will be prescribed. Chloroquine should not be taken by pregnant women. While anti-malarial preparations are available cheaply in India, courses should begun before arrival. Seek a home consultation as soon as your plans are known to give yourself plenty of time for vaccinations to become effective.

Rabies has not been eradicated in India and it is fatal. Keep away from all animals, including cute monkeys. If you are bitten by any creature, clean the wound well and go to a city hospital for injections. Private, Christian hospitals have the highest standards.

Take note of the generic names of any prescription drugs to show to a pharmacist in case you run out or lose them. Most 5-star hotels have drugstores but preparations may be under different brand names. If you are not staying at a 5-star, head for one if you need assistance. English will be spoken.

Ask your doctor to prescribe medications against most unfortunate contigencies. Your kit should include preparations for diahhorea, constipation, nausea and vomiting and a broad spectrum antibiotic against the type of infections you could pick up at home. Include analgesics, anti-malarials, which you'll continue to take during your visit, insect repellent (mosquito deterrent,) bandaids and anticeptic cream.

Do not bring narcotic drugs to India.

Despite tales of Delhi diahhorea and Bombay belly, you can enjoy India without being ill if you take adequate precautions. If you are unaccustomed to spicy food, introduce it to your system gradually. NEVER drink water that is not bottled mineral water or which has not been solidly boiled. Some big hotels have purified water on tap. Others may offer water that has been filtered but not boiled. Ask.

Practical Information

Ancient Shrine

Entry Regulations

See above under Documents

Customs

At Bombay's Sahar international airport, there is a red, something-to-declare lane and a green 'nothing to declare' lane. On arrival, your declaration may be verbal or you may be required to give up a form stating your agreement to re-export valuables such as jewellery, cameras etc. You may

Practical Information

be required to present all your baggage to be x-rayed before you LEAVE Bombay airport so that what you are importing can be determined - but neither situation always applies.

Duty Free Imports

Visitors to India for from between 24 hours and six months, provided not more than six visits are made in one year, can import personal belongings, including clothing, jewellery, one camera, one video-camera. one musical instrument, one radio, one tape recorder, a portable typewriter and sports equipment. Travel souvenirs must not exceed the value of 500 rupees duty free, regardless of the type of visa issued. Visitors of Indian origin can import these goods to the value of 1,000 rupees.(The extra is allowed for gifts to families.) A firearm may be imported provided a possession licence gained in advance or proof of exemption is produced.

Importation of pets is permitted with a combined health and rabies exemption certificate from a qualified veterinarian issued no more than a week before arrival.

Cigarettes: 200 or 50 cigars or 250 grammes of tobacco.
Alcohol: 1 bottle (.95 litre.)
Perfume: 2 oz.
Cologne: one quarter litre.

Goods in excess of the maximum permitted are subject to 325 per cent import duty unless the re-exportation guarantee has been signed. Visitors under age 17 may import one quarter of the adult allowance.

Currency

Unlimited currency may be imported provided an excess of US1000 is declared. Import and export of Indian rupees is prohibited. Money should be changed only at recognized banks and official money changers and receipted. Insist on a receipt if it is not given as it is necessary to produce this evidence in order to re- exchange rupees for foreign currency on leaving India.

Foreign travellers, including those of Indian origin, must pay major expenses including hotel accounts, airline fares and special train tickets in foreign currency or by foreign credit card. The rupee is the Indian unit, comprised of 100 paise.

Practical Information

> **INFOTIP:** When changing money, request notes of low denominations so that you have plenty of small tipping money.

Getting to India

By Air:

India is connected by air from all parts of the world. Flights may be through or via transfer connections to connecting airports. There are also many air charters.

By Rail:

In the past, it has been possible to enter India from Pakistan with lots of hassles but check with the Government of India Tourist Office on political relationships between the two countries in advance.

By Road:

The traditional land route from Europe via France, Germany, Yugoslavia, Bulgaria, Turkey, Iran and Pakistan has for some years been inadvisable for private motorists because of political turmoil in countries adjacent to this route. A few overland bus tours are still operated intermittently from London and inquiries should be made with GITO or major travel agents such as Thomas Cook and American Express. The automobile associations of western countries should be approached by any private motorists to obtain current information on the advisability of attempting the journey alone.

By Sea:

India is no longer connected by regular passenger ship services to western countries but several cruise lines include major Indian ports on some of their round-the-world itineraries. Inquiries should be made of major travel agents. However, some freighter lines which do call at major Indian ports such as Bombay, Calcutta and Madras offer limited passenger accommodation. These lines include the British India Steam Navigation Company and the American President Lines. Private yachtsmen need valid ship's documents.

Practical Information

> **INFOTIP:** Ensure the wine waiter does not bring your bottle uncorked. There will be no tampering with the contents but a bottle of claret could very well be labelled riesling and vice versa. You should be able to tell by the colour of the contents and send it back before it is opened - which may cost you if it is.

Electricity

The electric current in India is 220/250 volts and 50 cycles. It is AC almost everywhere.

Entertainment

Art Galleries and Museums

Bombay has several major museums and art galleries as has been discussed earlier in this book. Goa's are also listed here.
Jehangir Art Gallery, Mahatma Gandhi Rd., Tel: 243989.
Aakar Art Gallery, Bhulabhai Desai Rd., Tel: 8229778.
Chemould Art Gallery, Mahatma Gandhi Rd., Tel: 244356.
Coomaraswamy Hall, Prince Of Wales Museum, Mahatma Gandhi Rd., Tel: 244484.
Cymroza Art Gallery, 72 Bhulabhai Desai Rd., Tel: 8221755.
Pundole Art Gallery, Hutatma Chowk (Flora Fountain), Tel: 8221755.
Taj Art Gallery, Taj Mahal Hotel, Apollo Bunder, Tel: 2023366.
Centaur Art Gallery, Centaur Hotel, near Santacruz Airport, Tel: 6126660.
Conntempora Art Gallery, 9A Owen Dunn Rd., (off Hughes Rd.) Tel: 8223535.
Vithal's Workshop (owned by sculptor B. Vithal), 7 Raheja Centre, 214 Nariman Point, Tel: 232135.
Bajaj Art Gallery, Nariman Point, Tel: 2021359.
Gallery 7, Dhannur Building, Sir P.M. Rd., Tel: 258412, 250834.
Max Mueller Gallery, Max Mueller Bhavan, Museum Annexe, off Mahatma Gandhi Rd., Tel: 244710.
JJ Art Gallery, JJ School of Art and Architecture, Dadabhoy Naoroji Rd., Tel: 261652.
Prithvi Art Gallery, Prithvi Theatre, Janki Kutir, Juhu, Tel: 620969.

Practical Information

Street scene with pony cart

Jehangir Nicholson Museum of Modern Art, The National Centre For The Performing Arts, Dorabji Tata Rd., Nariman Point, Tel: 233737.
Mani Bhavan (Mahatma Gandhi Memorial Museum), 19, Laburnum Rd., Tel: 82227864.
The Prince of Wales Museum, Mahatma Gandhi Rd., behind Jehangir Art Gallery, Tel: 244519.
The Victoria and Albert Museum (Dr Bhau Daji Lad Museum), Jijamata Udyan, Byculla, Tel: 8723578.
Nehru Science Museum, Lala Lajpat Rai Rd., Tel: 493266
F.D. Alpiwalla Museum, Khareghat Memorial Hall, Khareghat (Parsi) Colony, Hughes Rd.
National Maritime Museum, 'Middle Ground,' off Gateway Of India.
Open Saturday, Sunday and public holidays only. Inquire of boat operators at Gateway Of India.

Practical Information

Goa Museums and Art Galleries

Archaeological Museum and Portrait Gallery, Old Goa, Tel: 5941. Archives Museum of Goa, Ashirwad Building, 1st Floor, Sant Inez, Panaji, Tel: 6006.

Children's Entertainment
Bombay and Goa

Children's Science Park, Nehru Science Centre and Planetarium, Lala Lajpat Rai Rd., Tel: 493266⅞.
Kamla Nehru Park, Bal Gangadhar Kher Rd., Malabar Hill.
Taraporewala Aquarium, Marine Drive.
Lion Safari Park, Sanjay Gandhi National Park, Borivli.
Victoria Gardens (elephant, camel and donkey rides and zoo,) Dr Babasaheb Ambedkar Rd.

There are a few parks situated around Bombay. Many of the attractions suitable for adults will also be of interest to children, including beaches already discussed.
Goa Children's Park, Municipal Garden, Menezes Braganza Park, Panaji.

Babysitting: Inquire from Housekeeping at your hotel.

Practical Information

Cinemas

As Bombay is the core of the world's film-making industry, there are many cinemas in the city and suburbs. However few of the productions are in English, so it is wise to check English language newspaper advertisements for those which are in English or have English sub-titles.

Bombay's major cinemas are:

- Akashwani, Churchgate Reclamation
- Apsara, Lamington Rd Eros, Churchgate
- Liberty, New Marine Lane
- Metro, Dhobi Talao
- New Empire, Victoria Terminus
- New Excelsior, Off D.N. Rd.
- Regal, Colaba Causeway
- Sterling, Victoria Terminus
- Alankar, S.V. Patel Rd.
- Apsara, Prarthan Samaj
- Dreamland, New Charni Rd
- Strand, Colaba
- Ganga-Jamuna, Tardeo
- Minerva, Lamington Rd.
- Imperial, Lamington Rd.
- Naaz, Lamington Rd.
- Maratha Mandir, Bombay Central
- Roxy, Charni Rd.
- Satyam/Sachinam/Sunderam, Worli
- Shalimar, Grant Rd.
- Novelty, Grant Rd and New Talkies, Bandra.

> **INFOTIP:** Because Bombayites are such keen movie buffs, it is wise to gain your cinema tickets in advance to avoid long, jostling queues and possible disappointment.

Cinemas in Goa

As Goa, with its historical buildings and quaint streets is often chosen as a movie setting, the Goanese are also movie enthusiasts. Cinemas are as follows:

- Cine Samrat Ashok, Panaji
- Cine El Dorado, Panaji
- Cine National, Panaji
- Cine Vasco, Vasco da Gama
- El Monte, Vasco da Gama
- Cine Lata, Margao
- Cine Metropole, Margao
- Cine Alankar, Mapusa and El Capotan, Mapusa.

Practical Information

Dance

Ballet:
 Homi Bhabba Auditorium, Navy Nagar, Colaba, Tel: 219111

Folk:
 NCPA Mini Theatre, Nariman Point, Tel: 234678. Shanmukhananda Hall, King Circle, Tel: 483978. (Music/dance theatre generally by visiting troupes in Tamil, Marathi, Malayalam and Kannada).
Prithvi Theatre, near Horizon Hotel, Juhu, Tel: 620969. (Dance and theatre in Hindi and English).
Patkar Hall, New Marine Lines, Tel: 253892 (dance qawali performances and English and Gujarati theatre).
Rang Bhavan, Dhobi Talao, Tel: 4150460 (Indian and Western music and Marathi theatre. Also contact for information on current cultural programmes and films.)

Koli dance:
 This characteristically lively dance of the Koli fisherwomen is special to Bombay. Check cultural programmes listed in the English language newspapers and cultural programmes offered by leading hotels during your stay.

Exhibitions

Exhibitions and trade fairs are frequently located in Bombay. For current information on what's on during your visit, contact Indian Merchants Chambers, 76 Veer Nariman, Tel: 296633. For Goa information, see BUSINESS GUIDE.

Practical Information

Cobra in a basket

Festivals

Bombay has a wide variety of festivals, each of which is celebrated in a distinctive way by religious groups or on special days of State or national occasion. Everyone joins in and visitors are welcome to participate.

Here is the annual calendar. Dates alter slightly from year to year, so check with GITO or your travel agent.

JANUARY: Makar Sankranti is colourful with flying kites. Relatives and friends exchange gifts to mark the winter solstice. Republic Day, January 26 is celebrated as a national festival throughout India. It marks the adoption of India's constitution.

FEBRUARY/MARCH: Mahashivratri or Shivrati is a solemn festival devoted to the worship of one of the Hindu trinity, Lord Shiva. The one-day event is celebrated by religious ceremonies continuing through the night and the singing of devotional songs. There are processions to

Practical Information

temples where mantras are chanted and lingams are annointed.

MARCH/APRIL: Holi is a boisterous festival observed all over India. People throw coloured water and powder over each other to celebrate the advent of Spring.

Gudi Padva is an auspicious New Year's day for the people of the State of Maharashtra to begin new ventures. Jamshedji Navroz is New Year's day for the Parsi community who adhere to the Falsi calendar and celebrate with feasting. Ramnavami is the birthday of the Hindu hero, Lord Rama, one of 10 incarnations of Lord Vishnu. There are celebrations in his honour. Good Friday is observed by all Indian Christians.

Mahavir Jayanti is the birthday of the 24th and last Jain tirthankara.

APRIL/MAY: Shivaji Jayanti is the birthday of Chatrapati Shivaji, the legendary king from Maharashtra. It is celebrated with functions in his honour all over Bombay.

Id-Ul-Fita (Ramzan Id) marks with feasting and rejoicing the end of Ramzan, the Muslim time of fasting.

Buddh Purnima is Buddha's birthday.

JULY/AUGUST: Naag Panchami is when live cobra (naag) or their images, are worshipped. There are religious ceremonies and milk offering made to live cobra.

Id-ul-Zuha (Bakr-Id) is the Muslim day observed to commemorate the prophet Ibrahim's sacrifice of his son in obedience to a command of God. Prayers are offered and alms given to the poor.

Independence Day is celebrated on August 15, the anniversary of India's freedom, won on this day in 1947.

Janamashtami, or Gokul Ashtami, is the birthday of Lord Krishna and fun to watch as energetic young men form human pyramids to release earthern pots filled with curds, suppposedly Lord Krishna's favourite sweets, which are strung high across the streets.

Coconut Day celebrates the end of the monsoon with fisherpeople venturing out to sea after offering coconuts to the sea god to ensure a good season. Friends exchange sacred threads and at public places recitations from the Hindu scriptures are made.

AUGUST/SEPTEMBER: Ganesh Chaturthi is the birthday of the elephant-headed god, Ganesh. This is one of Bombay's most impressive and colourful festivals and the city is one India's best centres to witness it. Big decorated images of the elephant god are worshipped, then carried with pomp in processions to be immersed in river or sea.

Mount Mary's Feast is the Christian feast of Our Lady of the Mount and is celebrated at the church of the same name in Vandra which also hosts a week-long fair.

Practical Information

SEPTEMBER/OCTOBER: Dussehra or Navratri is a 10-day time of great festival in which nine nights are spent in the worship of Devi, the mother goddess of the Hindus. Temporary shrines are built for public worship. Huge fairs are held and the Gujarati community performs Garba and Raas dances day and all night. The festival is based on the epic story of Ramayana and signifies the triumph of good over evil. It culminates in the destruction of effigies of Ravana, who was the epitomy of evil, by Rama, the god-hero.

Gandhi Jayanti is Mahatma Gandhi's birthday on October 2 and is celebrated with reverence, throughout India.

OCTOBER/NOVEMBER: Diwali is India's brightest festival. Each village, town and city becomes a fairyland of candles, lamps and millions of electric lights illuminating homes and public buildings. The goddess of wealth and prosperity, Laxmi, is worshipped and it is fitting that this signifies the New Year for the business community when new account books are opened. This Hindu festival of lights, also celebrates the homecoming of Lord Rama after a 14-year exile. There are fireworks everywhere.

Guru Nanak Jayanti is, on November 13, the birthday of the founder of Sikhism and a day of devotion by Bombay's Sikh community.

DECEMBER: Christmas Day on December 25 is the celebration of the birth of Jesus Christ and accompanied by traditional exchanges of goodwill greetings and gifts.

Practical Information

Festivals in Goa

National, religious and birthday events are also celebrated in Goa along with Hindu and Muslim festival days throughout the year. But of special significance are the Christian feast days. The most spectacular of Goa's social yearly events is Carnival or **Mardi Gras** a three-day legacy from the Portugese, beginning on a Saturday and finishing on the Tuesday before Ash Wednesday - the start of Lent. Everyone, regardless of religion, joins in masked balls, street dancing and parades in which colourful floats are pulled or driven through the streets. Groups of actors and musicians perform felos or plays with song, music and dance in the villages.

> **INFOTIP:** As the Christian calendar alters yearly, check that the dates of the pre-Lenten festival coincide with your visit. Mardi Gras in Goa is not to be missed.

Other Christian feast days of note are:

JANUARY 6: Feast Of The Three Kings, celebrated at Cuelim Chandler and with a fair at Reis Magos, which is near Fort Aguada.

FEBRUARY 2: Feast Of Our Lady Of Candelaria Pomburpa. Monday after the fifth Sunday in Lent. There is a procession at Velha Goa of 26 statues from Saint Andrews Church, all saints of the Franciscan third order, the only one outside Rome. There is also a large fair.

Sixteen days after Easter, the Feast Of Our Lady Of Miracles, is also celebrated by Hindus in honour of the Goddess Lairaya with a fair and market at Mapusa.

AUGUST 21 - 24: Festival of Novidades includes offering the first rice crop sheaves to the Head of State and a historical re-enactment.

DECEMBER 3: Feast of Saint Francis Xavier, Goa's patron saint at Old Goa.

DECEMBER 8: Feast of Our Lady of Immaculate Conception at Panaji and Margao.

DECEMBER 25: Christmas Day is celebrated throughout Goa by all sections of the community.

Seminars

Details of seminars and workshops will be found in Bombay's English language daily press. Check for details.

Practical Information

Radio/Television

Bombay radio: Vividhbharti - commercial radio. Bombay A -some transmissions in English. Bombay B - transmissions in all regional languages.

Television: Bombay Doordarshan - shared channel with other cities in mixed languages. Breakfast session 7 a.m. to 8 a.m. Afternoon: 1.45 p.m. to 2.45 p.m. Evening: 6 p.m. to varied end of transmission.

Theatre and Music

See also Dance

The National Centre for Performing Arts at Nariman Point hosts a wide variety of theatre, dance and musical performances, particularly by foreign orchestras, troupes and players in the monsoon season. Check the newspapers for details.

Tata Theatre is the centre's major auditorium which presents theatre from across the country and abroad. Tel: 234678.

Practical Information

Birla Matushri Sabhagriha, New Marine Lines, Tel: 296707, has Gujarati, Marathi and Hindi theatre, Indian music concerts and the occasional English musical.
Sahitya Sangh Mandir, Charni Rd., Tel: 351088, presents Marathi and Gujarati theatre and Indian music concerts.

Tejpal Auditorium, Gowalia Tank, Tel: 8227579, has theatre in English, Gujarati and Hindi.

Sophia Bhabha Auditorium, Bhulabhai Desai Rd., Tel: 8228450, has English theatre and western musicals and concerts.

Getting Around Bombay

Bombay claims the best public transport system of any city in India. But the crowds on it can be a deterrent, particularly at peak periods.

Bus:

The double-decker buses a la the streets of London are quite reasonably maintained and are operated by Bombay Electric Supply and Transport. You can pick them up from Victoria Railway Station and Bombay Central to central points in a wide network covering city and suburbs. Or inquire of BEST on 8828739.

Practical Information

Train:

Unlike in other cities in India, Bombay's train system is worth trying but not at peak hours when literally millions of commuters are using the facility. The Dadar - Bombay Central - Churchgate line with many stations in between will be the main route suitable for most visitors. You can travel first or second class but as the fares are so cheap, the former is advisable - although you probably will not get a seat anyway! Inquiries: VT -2043535, Dadar - 4224161, Bombay Central - 4933535

Taxis:

While many taxis are metered, just as many are not. If the taxi has a meter, insist on it being flagged as soon as you enter. Where there is no meter in taxi or auto rickshaw, (a funny little three-wheeled vehicle which will be cheaper than a normal car,) ask to see the latest fare chart which the driver should have.

Taxis are plentiful in Bombay and can be hailed off the street. But if you want one that is air conditioned, order it from your hotel front desk or from the doorman outside. In the better class of hotel, the doorman controls incoming taxis and limousines with microphone and/or whistle.

> **INFOTIP:** If the taxi is unmetered and/or the driver does not speak English, ask your hotel doorman the fare you can expect to pay at your destination, and, if necessary, that he instruct the driver exactly where you want to go.

Always negotiate the fare on an unmetered taxi before you start off if you have flagged one down in the street. Do not hire a tourist taxi or limousine for an excursion from an unlicenced or unapproved operator. GITO or your hotel will assist in finding a reputable firm. See Rental Vehicles with Drivers in this section. These firms have been approved by GITO.

> **INFOTIP:** As you leave Bombay International Airport, you will be beseiged by dozens of drivers wanting to take you to the city. Head for a booth which sells fixed price taxi tickets instead. If you have difficulty locating it on the left hand side of the exit door, ask any airport worker for its location.

If you are travelling by taxi late at night you may have difficulty in getting a driver to turn on the meter. Again insist on a price before you commence the trip.

Practical Information

Getting Around Outside Bombay

By Road:

As in Bombay itself, you can travel to its outskirts and well beyond by road by six methods.
1. Unmetered or private taxis. Fix rates in advance.
2. Metered taxis or auto rickshaws, usually painted yellow and black. Ask for the rate card in case the meter is not correctly calibrated for new rates, which is not uncommon.
3. Tourist cars/taxis, usually Indian Ambassador cars, which are quite comfortable and mostly chauffeur-driven by an English speaking driver. Some of these vehicles are air conditioned. Rates are reasonable and can be negotiated on an hourly or daily basis or for specific journeys. Alternatively the rate can be fixed per kilometre.
4. Limousine (luxury car/taxi.) These are imported air conditioned vehicles with English-speaking chauffeurs. The manner in which rates are determined is as above.
These vehicles are available in Bombay and other major cities, but not in small towns. 5. Coaches for groups can be hired via the nearest Tourist Office.
6. 'Luxury' bus services to and from tourist centres. As schedules of these vehicles change, contact GITO for current departure times and places.

By Rail:

There are five classes of accommodation in Indian trains but it is recommended that visitors travel First Class air conditioned or First Class which is about half price of air conditioned.

Practical Information

Maharashtra Tourist Development Corporation, CDO Hutments, Madame Cama Road, near LIC Building, Tel: 2026713. For information on tours, Tel: 241713, 241762.

Driving Yourself:

Currently, India has no rental car facilities but they are planned soon to be introduced. Visitors may import their own vehicles but they must be covered by Triptyques or Carnets issued by an internationally recognised automobile association or club affiliated with the Aliiance Internationale de Tourism, Geneva. Vehicles are allowed free of import duty for six months. Vehicles imported under Customs Carnets are permitted mainly for holiday-makers. The vehicle must be re-exported. Obtain an International Certificate for Motor Vehicles from your own country's automobile association or club, also an International Driving Permit.

Visitors intending to import a vehicle should write first to Western India Automobile Association, Lalji Narainji Memorial Building, 76, Veer Nariman Rd., Bombay, 400020. Tel: 2041085. Particularly if the vehicle is arriving by sea, the association can help in clearing vehicles, payment of service charges, Port Trust wharfage and documentation.

A third party insurance is necessary for all vehicles (also canoes less than 5.5 metres long,) before use. Insurance must be paid to a company registered in India or a foreign company with a guarantor in India. In India, vehicles are driven on the left hand side of the road.

By Air:

If you are travelling large distances from Bombay, flying is undoubtedly the way to go. The Indian domestic airline, Indian Airlines, the largest carrier in south Asia, has an extensive network throughout the country. A second airline called Vayudoot also operates some services not previously included by Indian Airlines and duplicates others on high traffic routes.

Visitors to India must buy their air tickets in foreign currency. Indian Airlines has several special fares for tourists from abroad. These include:

1. Discover India (21 days of unlimited travel provided no city is touched more than once except to transfer or connect.)

2. Tour India (Travel anywhere domestically for a maximum of six flights within 14 days. No city can be touched more than once, except to transfer or connect.)

3. India Wonderfares (Four fares each permitting unlimited travel for one week within north, south, east or west India regions. No city can be touched more than once except to transfer or connect. Cities included in the western region

Practical Information

are Bombay, Ahmedabad, Aurangabad, Belgaum, Bhavnagar, Bhug, Goa, Indore, Jamnagar, Jodphur, Mangalore, Nagpur, Nasik, Pune, Rajkot, Udaipur and Vadodare.)

4. Youth Fares (25 per cent discount on US $ airfare on domestic and Indo - Nepal sectors for persons between 12 and 30 years of age.)

These economical packages can be bought abroad through Air India.

Reservations: Indian Airlines, Air India Building, Nariman Point, Bombay, Tel: 2023031, 2042500.

> **INFOTIP:** You must confirm all flights as soon as possible as there are more passengers than aeroplanes! Make your first task on arrival at a new destination in India to confirm your flight out. You will be required to be at the airport at least two hours before the flight, even though the check-in desk may not open until a short time before the flight is due to leave. Queue your luggage, find a seat and never take your eyes off your suitcases.

Vayudoot's network is less than Indian Airlines and subject to change. Currently it operates passenger services from Bombay to Goa via Pune and also from Bombay to Aurangabad. For information contact GITO, Bombay or Vayudoot Ltd., Malhotra Building, F Block, Janpath, New Delhi 110 001, Tel: 3312587, 3312779, 3315768.

Air India also operates some internal flights between major cities, i.e. Delhi - Bombay. Air India links Goa with Kuwait via Trivandrum. The airline's Goa office is at Dempo House, Bandodkar Road, Campal, Panaji, Tel: 3826, 3831, 4067 or at Dabolim Airport, Tel: 2788.

Sahar International Airport is about 5 km from Santacruz Domestic Airport, Bombay. A shuttle bus leaving about every 30 minutes operates between the two airport terminals 24 hours a day. From both airports coaches depart for the city and usually include major hotels enroute. Departures from Terminal 2 (International) are every hour from 2 a.m. to 5 a.m. and 7 a.m. to 11 p.m. Departures from Terminal 1 (domestic) are every hour from 2.30 a.m. to 5.30 a.m. and 7.30 a.m. to 11 p.m.

At both terminals GITO maintains an office to assist travellers, at Sahar, open 24 hours.

Passengers are required to pay a travel tax of 30 rupees before each internal flight and Foreign Travel Tax of 100R on leaving India. You can change money back into foreign currency at Sahar Airport on production of exchange receipts.

Practical Information

The Indrail Pass can be purchased with foreign currency by overseas visitors. This pass allows unlimited travel by rail within the period of validity and it can be bought at the Railway Central Reservation Office in Bombay (Railway Tourist Guide, Central Railway, Victoria Terminus and Railway Tourist Guide, Western Railway, Churchgate Station. The pass is also sold at the Central Reservation Office, Vasco da Gama Station in Goa.)

The pass is good value if you are travelling continuously.

Holding a pass does not guarantee you a seat, so make a reservation. This comes without fee to pass holders, along with sleeper charges and supplementary charges for fast trains. Ordinary ticket-holders pay these fees. The time expended in gaining reservations can be frustrating. Make reservations up to six months in advance, if possible. If you book through a reputable travel agency with expertise in India, you can book your reservations in advance from home. A reservation ticket shows your seat/berth and carriage.

Do not expect Western First Class in sleeping compartments which usually transform into normal compartments by day. Bed rolls are provided in the AC class and on certain first class routes for a small fee, also in some second class sleepers. Tourists can reserve retiring rooms at railway stations for no more than 72 hours from occupation. Apply to individual station masters.

An Indrail Pass gives use of station waiting rooms - and their toilets. Use these in preference to those on board, which are often dirty.

Also available is the Indrail Rover Ticket for a selection

Practical Information

of 32 itineraries of seven, 15, 21 and 30 days.

If you do not want an Indrail Pass or Rover Pass you can buy standard circular journey tickets which include a large number of stations. These are sold by each zonal railway and do away with the need to buy tickets at each stage. Travelling from Bombay to Vasco da Gama in Goa takes about 24 hours and you must change trains at Miraj. If you are going east to Aurangabad, the 10-hour trip includes a change at Manmad.

Tickets can be bought and reservations made at the railway office which is right next to the Government of India Tourist Office, 123 M. Karve Road, Bombay, just opposite Churchgate Station. Also Victoria Terminus Station, Tel: 2043535, 2047655, between 8 a.m. and 1 p.m. and 2 p.m. and 8 p.m. Seek assistance here from the Railway Tourist Guide.

For details and bookings of Indrail Passes contact the following general sales agents in your own country:
Australia: Adventure World Pty. Ltd., 37 York Street, Sydney, NSW, Tel: (02) 2903222: Penthouse Travel Pty. Ltd., 72 Pitt Street, Sydney, NSW, Tel: (02) 2311455.
Canada: Hariworld Travels Inc., Royal York Hotel, 100 Front Street West, Arcade Level, Toronto, Ontario M5J 1E3, Tel: 3662000.
Japan: Japan Travel Bureau, Overseas Travel Division, 1-6 - 4 Marunouchi, Chiyoda KU, Tokyo 100, Tel: 81 - (031) 2847391.
United Kingdom: S. D. Enterprises Ltd., 21 York House, Empire Way, Wembley, Middx, HA9 OPA,
Tel: 019033411, 012009549.
USA: Hariworld Travels Inc., 30 Rockefeller Plaza, Shop 21, North Mezanine, New York, NY 10112, Tel: (212) 9573000.
Hong Kong: Thomas Cook Travel Servixces, 6/F D'Aguiler Place, 1-13, D'Aguiler St., Central, Hong Kong.

By Bus:

Generally in India bus travel is faster than rail, particularly, for example, on the Bombay - Goa run. See Goa section of this guide.

It is preferable not to travel alone on a bus as close check should be maintained on luggage which is usually placed on top of the bus. Chai (tea) stops are frequent as indeed are unscheduled stops and there is a continuous stream of passengers taking luggage on and off. On some routes you can reserve a seat. At some bus stations there is a separate queue for women.

Inquiries: Maharashtra State Road Transport Corporation, Central Bus Stand, Bombay Central, or Parel Depot, Sanghi Motors, Pty. Ltd., 39A Hughes Road, Bombay,
Tel: 353598.

Practical Information

Help

Consulates

Consular activities are listed below. These services exist by agreement with the Government of India and are bound by certain Indian regulations, as well as by orders from their home countries.

Questions regarding:
- Visas and passports
- Citizenship, dual nationality, national status
- Military service status of dual-nationality persons
- Difficulties with local regulations (Customs, the law, etc.)
- Assistance with absentee voting in home country
- Notarization or witnessing of documents
- Assistance in the case of a death
- Assistance with repatriation problems

Consulates are supposed to be notified in case of hospitalization of a foreigner, if the nationality of the patient is known.

In case of arrest in India, your consulate should be notified. Both Indians and foreigners are subject to the same laws in India and ignorance of the law is not a grounds for defence. However the consulate may inform you of your rights, notify your family, register complaints on your behalf and try to contact one of the Indian organisations that visit prisons and are concerned with the welfare of prisoners.

Australia: Maker Tower E, 16th floor, Cuffe Parade, 217366.

Austria: Taj Building, Dadabhai Naoroji Rd., 2042044.

Bahrain: Maker Tower F, Cuffe Parade, 216114

Belgium: 'Morena', 11 M.L. Dahanukar Marg, 4929261.

Canada: Malhotra House, Opp. GPO, 261240/265219.

Cyprus: The Drawing Room Ltd, 14 Dubash Marg, 224294/242986.

Denmark: L&T House, Ballard Estate, 268181.

Egypt: 12/B Maker Tower, 1st floor, Cuffe Parade, 212425/217555.

Federal Republic of Germany: Hoechst House, 10th floor, Nariman Point, 232422/232517.

Finland: The Times of India, D.N. Rd., 267273.

France: Hongkong Bank Building, Mahatma Gandhi Rd., 271528/271493.

Greece: Ralli House, Damodardas Sukhadwala Marg, 2048221.

Iceland: 38, Western India House, Sir Pherozshah Mehta Rd., 251931.

Indonesia: Lincoln Annexe, S. Barodawala Marg, 368678/381051.

Ireland: Royal Bombay Yacht Club, Apollo Bunder, 2023774/2027052.

Italy: Vaswani Mansion, D. Wachha Rd, 222192/222748.

Japan: 1, M.L. Dahanukar Marg, 4923847/4924610.

Netherlands: The International, 16 M. Karve Rd, 296840.

Norway: Naoroji Mansion, Nathalal Parekh Marg, 242042.

Philipines: Industry House, J. Tata Rd, 2026340.

Portugal: Moti Mahal, J. Tata Rd, 2026340.

Spain: 6, K. Dubash Marg, 244644.

Sweden: Indian Mercantile Chambers, R. Kamani Marg, 262583/269483.

Switzerland: Manek Mahal, Veer Nariman Rd., Churchgate, 293550/294003.

United Kingdom: (Deputy High Commission). Hongkong Bank Building, Mahatma Gandhi Rd., 274874.

U.S.A.: Lincoln House, 78 Bhulabhai Desai Rd, 8223611/8.

Yugoslavia: Vaswani Mansion, D. Wachha Rd, 222050/222373.

Practical Information

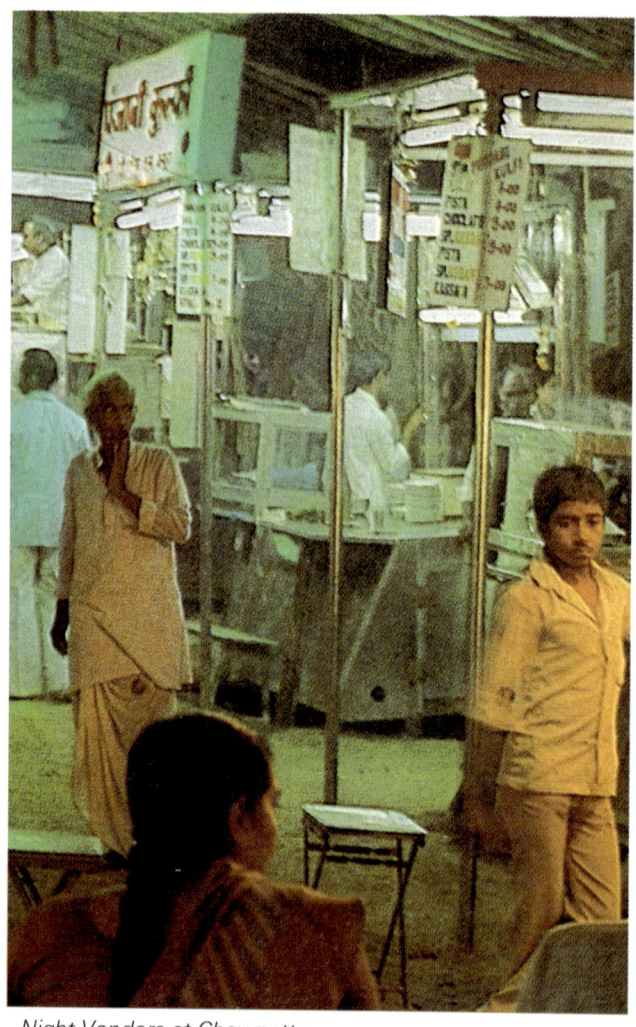
Night Vendors at Chowpatty

Medical Emergencies

There are two important telephone numbers in **Bombay** for medical emergencies:

Ambulance: dial 102.
Police: 100.

Most five, four and three star hotels have direct associations with a nearby medical practice and will assist in arranging a medical consultation in your hotel room should you become ill.

Hospitals and nursing homes in the Bombay central area

Practical Information

are as follows:
Bombay Hospital, Marine Lines, Tel: 297100/297720.
Bombay Port Trust Hospital, Antop Hull Rd., Tel: 4129684/4127947.
Breach Candy Hospital, Warden Rd.,
Tel: 8223651/8229501.
Cooper Hospital, Juhu ara Rd. Tel: 6124312/6367330.
J.J. Hospital, Mohammad Ali Rd., Tel: 860943/869400.
Jaslok Hospital, 15 Peddar Rd., Tel: 4944460/4944464.
K.E.M. Hospital, Parel, Tel: 4136051.
M.A. Poddar Hospital, Worli, Tel: 4933593.
Nair Hospital, near Bombay Central Railway Station,
Tel: 391491.

Goa

Ambulance: Telephone 5926, 22164, 2211 and 2454.

Goa is well-serviced with hospitals and medical clinics. Your hotel will advise on the closest and best. Four include Gosalia Memorial Hospital and Research Institute, Dr. E. Beges Rd, Dona Paula, Tel: 3814. C. M. M. Polyclinic, Altinhe, Panaji.Tel: 5918. Dr. J.J. Costa Hospital, Fatorda, Margao. Tel: 22586. Hospital de Hospicio, Margao. Tel: 22164.

If you must be admitted to hospital, your consulate will give advice on how to handle payment.

Should you require non-prescription medicines, or need to have a script made up from a doctor's prescription, here are several day and night pharmacies to contact in Bombay:

M/S Wordell, Chemist, Stadium House, Veer Nariman Rd, Tel: 220768.
M/S Bombay Medico, Bhatia General Hospital, Chikalwadi J. Dadajee Rd, Tel: 373614.
M/S Navjivan Chemist, S.K. Patil Hospital, 134 Daftary Rd, Malard, Tel: 694381.
M/S New Royal Chemist, Liberty Cinema, Building 41-42, New Marine Lines, Tel: 257929.
M/S Noble Chemist, Harkisondas Hospital Building, 123 New Charni Rd., Tel: 353130.

Police Emergencies

Death

A foreign visitor's death entails instant communication with his/her|consulate by|relatives, hotel personnel, friends, hospital or police authorities.

Practical Information

Lost Property

Should you lose something in your hotel, report it immediately to the hospitality desk if you are in a large hotel or front desk manager if in a smaller establishment. Otherwise contact the police.

Replacement of Items

In the event of losing your passport, report it to your consulate immediately. Guard your airline tickets as carefully as you would your cash. They will not be reissued.

Credit Cards: Report the loss immediately to the crediut card company concerned. Check with your hotel's front desk for current address and telephone numbers in Bombay.

Travellers' Cheques: Lost or stolen travellers cheques are usually replaced quickly by the issuing banks or agents but the swiftness of replacement may depend on what proof you can supply, particularly cheque numbers and receipt for their purchase. Keep these in a separate place in your luggage away from your cheques.

Railway Passes: A lost railway pass may be replaced at the discretion of the authority, particularly if the number of the pass can be confirmed with the railway office which issued it. Contact Victoria Terminus Railway Tourist Guide: Tel: 2043535.

CRIME

Unfortunately, theft and pickpocketing are common. If you are a victim, try to recall as much detail as possible. It is rare for a stranger to be molested although it is unwise to wander around at night by yourself and to give alms to one person in a group of beggars. Be watchful of your luggage just before leaving a station. Sometimes, groups of thieves operate at this time, tossing bags from the train as it departs.

Should your driver be involved in a motor accident in a village outside Bombay, do not attempt to stop him from leaving the scene. Urge him to go to the nearest police station. Tempers run high if anyone is injured, so his

Practical Information

escape is self-defence. The police will offer protection and also investigate. The police emergency telephone number is 100. For other police inquiries, contact: Commissioner of Police, Greater Bombay, Tel: 262826, 268111. Sahar Airport: 6323002, 6320812, 6324027. Santa Cruz Airport: 6141152, 6122131, 6149831. Other districts: Colaba, 2021122; Worli, 4930383; Dadar, 4223664; Bandra, 463021; Borivli, 662331.

Goa: Telephone 100 (emergency) or 22175, 22318 or 2504.

Motoring

See also section on getting around India by road. While it is not possible yet to rent a car in Bombay, motor cycles are for hire in Goa. Inquire there at the Directorate of Tourism, Tourist Home, Pato Bridge, Panaji, Tel: 5583, 5315, 4757.

Should you have your own vehicle, remember that throughout India traffic moves on the left side of the road and passes on the right side of a vehicle. There is no speed limit with the exception of 40 or 60 kilometres per hour as indicated in built- up city areas.

Most major roads are good but secondary roads are not of the same standards, particularly during the monsoon season. Gain information from Western India Automobile Association, Lalji Narainji Memorial Building, 76 Veer Nariman Rd, Bombay, Tel: 2041085 on whether roads, especially those with bridges are open.

Rental Vehicles With Drivers

There are many car hire firms in Bombay and a few in Goa. Most of them have offices in Central Bombay offering Ambassador cars, limousines and mini-coaches with drivers and with or without air conditioning. They include:
Autohirers, 7 Commerce Centre, Tardeo Rd.,
Tel: 4942006.
Blue Star Garage, Chinoy Mansion, off Warden Rd. Junction, Tel: 8221331.
India Tourism Development Corporation, Nirmal Building, Nariman Point, Tel: 2026679.
Maharashtra Tourism Development Corporation, CDO Hutments, Madame Cama Rd., Tel: 2026713.
Pravin Auto Hirers, Linking Rd., Santacruz, (limousines only,) Tel: 535896.

Practical Information

Starline Services, Arvind Kunj, Tardeo Main Rd., Tel: 4944637.
Trade Wings Ltd., 30, K Dubash Rd., Tel: 244334.
Travel Cars, G-9, Kalpataru, 39 Dr. G Deshmukh Rd., Tel: 4941083.

> **INFOTIP:** On country roads and to a lesser extent, in Bombay, there is an unwritten rule that trucks, closely followed by buses, have right of way, even to pass in the face of oncoming traffic. This they do with alarming regularity, forcing all other types of transport from camel and ox-drawn carts to limousines off the road. Drive as do the Indians, using your car horn continuously and flashing your headlights. Be prepared to get out of the way quickly.

Publications in English

English Language Booksellers

Government of India Tourist Office, 123 M. Karve Rd, opposite Churchgate Station, has plenty of literature in English on Bombay and most other parts of India.
The Oberoi Hotel, Nariman Point has an excellent bookshop as has its sister hotel
The Oberoi Towers, which stocks the A-Z of Bombay, a comprehensive road guide to the city.
The *Taj Mahal Hotel* has a good bookshop. *Chetana Restaurant*, 34 K. Dubash Rd., *Rampart Row*, has a wide selection of books on religious and philosophic themes. Also there is *Bookpoint, Ballard Estate* and Strand, near Sir P.M. Rd., behind Horniman's Circle and Flora Fountain. Most five star hotels have a kiosk in which English language books, non-fiction and fiction, magazines and newspapers are for sale.

Libraries With Books In English

Mani Bhavan, Mahatma Gandhi Memorial Museum, 19 Laburnum Rd. Royal Asiatic Society Library, off Horniman Circle.

Practical Information

Post Offices

Generally post and telegraph offices are open between 10 a.m. and 5 p.m. although there are services at the general post office outside of these hours. The post office at Sahar International airport is open 24 hours daily.

> **INFOTIP:** Envelopes on sale or available through your hotel are short on back adhering material. Glue is provided at most post offices but to make sure your letter is sealed, buy a roll of cellulose tape for more security.

Bombay's General Post Office, Nagar Chowk, has post restante facilities. There is also a Post Office counter at Santacruz domestic airport. Other main Post Offices include Churchgate, A Rd., Colaba Post Office, Colaba bus station and the Foreign Post Office at Ballard Pier. The Central Telegraph Office is at Hutatma Chowk and public facsimile facilities are available at MTNL, Telephone Bhavan, opposite the Strand Cinema. Colaba. Smaller Post and Telegraph offices are to be found all over Bombay and suburbs and 5-star hotels usually include them. If not, the front desks of most 5 and 4 star hotels offer postal facilities for guests. The World Trade Centre, off Cuffe Parade, has a big post office.

Goa: General Post Office, Panaji. Tel: 3704. Telegraph Office, Dr. Atmaram Borcar Rd, Panaji. Tel 3742.

Practical Information

In Festival mood

Religious Services in English

Catholic

Holy Name Cathedral, N. Parekh Rd., Colaba. Tel: 2020121.
Our Lady of the Mount Church, Bandra. Tel: 533152.
Our Lady of Glory Church, Byculla. Tel: 376600.
St. Andrew's Church, Bandra. Tel: 533680.
St Michael's Church, Mahim. Tel: 354483.

Protestant

St Thomas Cathedral, Veer Nariman Rd.
St John's Church. Tel: 211217.

Practical Information

Jewish

Services may not be conducted in English.
Knesseth Eliyahoo, Fort.
Margen David, Byculla.
Margen Hasidim, Abdul Hamid Ansari Rd, near Jacob Circle.
Tifereth Israel, Clerk Rd, near Jacob Circle.

Goa

Services may not be in English.

Catholic

Our Lady of Immaculate Conception, Panaji.
Our Lady of Fatima, Panaji.
Our Lady of Immaculate Conception, Calangute.
Church of Our Lady of Miracles, Mapusa.
Our Lady of Immaculate Conception, Margao.
St Andrew's Church, Vasco da Gama.

Protestant

Christian Methodist Church, Panaji.
Ponda Chapel, near bus station, Ponda.

Restaurants and Nightlife

Bombay is not only a melting pot of almost all of India's cuisines but most of the world's as well. Its mixture of internal cultures and outside conquerors has resulted in the city being able to provide the greatest and most exciting variety of food in the sub-continent. So eat heartily though wean your system on to the spicier dishes if you are not used to them.

Prices, even in the five-star establishments, by western standards, are inexpensive and a good, non-hotel, simple eatery can provide terrific value for very little.

While it is believed that India's national dish is curry and rice, there is no such single thing as curry. It's as general as the word sauce. Curry is a combination of freshly ground spices, each able to be varied in intensity of palate heat and subtlety of flavour and combined with meat, fish, poultry or vegetables and, occasionally, fruit. Indian cooks may

Practical Information

select from about 25 different spices and many herbs to make what westerners recognise as curry. Many of the recipes are closely guarded secrets handed down from generation to generation. Spices are ground freshly or used whole. Some restaurants are classified purely as Indian. Here you'll be served a merge of styles that have become distinctively national.

Many of the top class hotels produce excellent European food and also authentic fare from other parts of Asia. But you won't be able to get a steak because the cow is sacred. A reasonable alternative in a few establishments is the buffalo steak and your hamburger is likely to be lamburger or burger made from ham as from the pig. The latter meat is considered unclean by Muslims.

> **INFOTIP:** If dining with a Muslim in a restaurant where pork is on the menu, ask if your choice of it will offend. If you think it might, opt for another type of meat.

Not all Hindus are strict vegetarians but because many are, it is likely you'll end up discovering a whole new world of vegetables in India. A strict Buddhist will not even eat eggs.

BREAKFAST: Most hotels serve western breakfast, continental and/or cooked with, often, a goodly selection of fruits as well. The toast might not be as you'd prepare it yourself and the bacon might be done to a crisp as Americans prefer it. (Specify otherwise if you don't like this.) The milk for your tea or coffee might be boiled and hot but it will be safe to drink. Otherwise you may be given powdered creamer. Generally, western breakfasts are hearty and good value.

You might like to try Indian-style breakfast, perhaps masala dosa, vegetable-stuffed pancakes served with pickles on a banana leaf, or rice with vegetables and pickles. These make interesting changes and hotels have selections on their menus for their Indian guests.

> **INFOTIP:** While it is doubtful that juice freshly squeezed in a good hotel will be contaminated, if you are at all hesitant about hygiene standards in your accommodation, order tinned juice.

Some hotels have 24-hour coffee shops in which case you'll have no problem in gaining breakfast if you have to be on the move before 7 a.m. when most hotel dining

Practical Information

rooms open for the first repast of the day. An alternative is 24-hour room service but you may find that only tea and coffee are available before this hour.

LUNCH AND DINNER: Bombayites start lunching between noon and 12.30 p.m. in restaurants, hotel or otherwise, and at any time from street vendors. Some (not in hotels) open as early as 11 a.m. and all continue till 3 p.m. at least. While many restaurants open for dinner from 7 to 7.30 p.m., those located in hotels tend to open at either 7.30 or 8 p.m

Because of the diversity of food in Bombay, here is a resume of the regional styles you are likely to encounter in hotel, restaurant or street stall in Bombay, also in Goa which has its own distinctive cuisine.

Northern Indian

The hearty food of the north has Muslim then Mughal influences resulting in the variety of savoury, rich lamb dishes based on cooking with ghee and cream. The cuisine was enhanced by the tandoor method of cooking which was indigenous to the north west frontier province, now Pakistan, and the Punjab. The tandoor is a clay oven which burns wood or charcoal and imparts an unparalleled smoky flavour to mildly-spiced, tender meats, fish, poultry and breads.

Punjabi food is simple and filling, an amalgamation of the cuisines of the Greeks, Persians, Afghans and Mongols, plus northern invaders. Ghee, fresh milk products and vegetables are utilized.

If you see a restaurant advertizing Frontier Food, it is likely to include tandoor and Punjabi food and is well worth experiencing. Here are some dishes to try:

Naan: Leavened flour bread
Biriyani: Rice, saffron and marinated lamb
Kabab: Meat, poultry or fish served on a skewer with accompaniments such as tomatoes, onion, capsicum.
Murgh: Chicken. Murgh tikka should be melt-in- the-mouth tandoori chicken morsels on a kebab.
Paneer: Cottage cheese. Palek Paneer is the cheese, spices, onion and tomato served with spinach. Matter paneer is with peas.
Pillau: Spiced rice
Keema: Minced meat
Roghan Josh: Lamb with spices in yoghurt

Practical Information

> **INFOTIP:** While cutlery will be supplied to visitors, it is acceptable to eat particularly frontier food with your right hand which adds another sensory perception to your enjoyment. Don't allow the food to rise up into your palm but use fingers. It's easy to become adept.

Maharashtrian

The cuisine of the State of which Bombay is capital is healthy and emphasizes wheat, rice, vegetables (many of the people are vegetarian,) nuts and nut oils, sesame seeds and coconut. Often, vegetables are spiced with a combination of ground and roasted cumin, sesame seeds, cardamom, cinnamon and coconut. Bombay Duck is Maharashtrian and is a little fish pickled, stewed or fried. Sweet and sour dishes are also interesting eating.

Specialties include the following snack which is best tried on Chowpatty or Juhu beaches from a Bombaywallah's stall. Bhel puri: Boiled potatoes, onion, fresh coriander, crisp wheat, puffed rice served with chutneys and chick pea vermicelli.

Gujarati

From the neighbouring State of Gujarat comes an interesting vegetarian cuisine, usually served thali style, ie on a tray with each different dish served in small stainless-steel bowls - a mini smorgasbord. The food is oil free and not pungent and the waiters keep filling up the thali bowls until you are replete. The cuisine is a trifle sweet and desserts, made often with milk and/or yoghurt, are special. To contrast, the Gujaratis are big on pickles and relishes.

Khandvi: Gram flour paste steamed rolls with mustard seed and fresh coriander.
Dhoklas: Steamed lentil cakes.

Note: Not all thali-food is vegetarian. It is a style of presentation rather than cuisine. Embracing several styles, a typical thali meal is meat, chicken or fish, two vegetable dishes, dhal or lentils pureed, raita (yoghurt mixed with cucumber or other vegetables to refresh the palate,) pickles or chutney and perhaps one of the breads - naan, papadams, roti or chapatti. Rice is also served.

Practical Information

Parsi

While Parsi food is heavily spiced, it is not overly hot which makes it a favourite with many foreigners. With a Persian heritage, the Parsis are into meat and fish and eggs.(If a Parsi is stumped for a culinary idea, he/she adds eggs.)

Dhansak: Traditionally eaten on Sundays, cooked in a mixture of several dhals (lentil sauces, common to many of India's cuisines,) chicken or lamb comes with deep fried meat balls and caramelized brown rice.

Patra-ni-Machini: Served on special occasions is this pomfret (fish) fillet, stuffed with coriander and coconut chutney and steamed in a banana leaf.

Sindhi

The Sindhis are a people who migrated from Pakistan after 1947 petition, bringing with them a little-known cuisine characterized by garlic and mint flavoured chutneys and pickles and sweets like mithais and hashwas. Food is not necessarily vegetarian.

Kofta Tas-Me: Meat balls in sauce of onion, tomato, chilli, ginger, coriander and sprinkled with garam masala.

Bengali

Fish, particularly freshwater, seafood, mustard seed and oil (grown in the region) dominate the Bengali diet which is rejecting of sea fish. Fish is stewed, grilled or fried. While yoghurt is rarely offered separately, it is used sometimes in preparation. A speciality from the days of the Raj is marinated hilsa but, beware, it has lots of bones. The Bengalis love sweetmeats.

Murhu Ghonta: Classic Bengali fish head, spicy.
Maacher Jhol: Lightly fried fish in a gravy westerners would classify as curry.

South Indian

In the south, one finds a Brahmin cuisine, distinctive because strict south Indian Brahmins will not eat tomatoes and beetroot because they are blood colour and neither onion nor garlic. Recipes are based on tamarind, chilli,

Practical Information

coconut and yellow lentil. These combined with a vegetable make sambhar, a staple dish eaten twice daily with rasama, a peppery, lentil based consumee and the basis of the English-inspired mulligatawny. With rice, vegetables, coconut and yoghurt, you have a typical meal.

The popularity of idlis and dosas, respectively steamed dumplings and pancakes made from fermented ground rice and dhal, has spread throughout the nation. Yet Moghul influences from Hyderabad, also those of Christian, Syrian, and Jewish origin are also prominent in the food and meat and seafood are enjoyed also by non-vegetarians. Some dishes can be exceedingly hot to western palates.

Haleem: Wheat and mutton.
Hyderabad biryani: Rice with meat.
Baghara baigan: Eggplant dish.

Goan

The Christian Portguese had a great influence on Goan cuisines as did the Muslims. Traditions of Christians using vinegar, Hindus lokum, a sour fruit and tamarind, to give pungency, combine with the Christian preference for pork and the non- vegetarian Hindus liking for lamb. Seafood and fish are bountiful. Goan sausages are richly individual (rather salty.)

Vindaloo: Meat in garlic spices and vinegar. (Whoosh! Have plenty of water ready.)
Sorpatel: Pork in a similar combo.
Fish or seafood curries: Self explanatory and very good.

Alcoholic Drinks

In the State of Maharashtra, of which Bombay is capital, there is partial prohibition of alcohol. While some visitors can travel in and out, drink alcohol freely in hotels and even buy it without being questioned in liquor stores, others may be asked to produce their All India Liquor Permits at the latter. Beer can be bought without the permit.

It is not traditional for alcohol to be served in other than westernized Indian homes and some restaurants serve only beer, in addition to fruit juices and water. Imported spirits and wines are served in top hotel restaurants but at astronomical prices.

Some Indian maitre d's seem rather reluctant to admit that India produces its own wine and spirits. Some of the wine is surprisingly good and some of it awful but so is

Practical Information

imported wine that has tainted while waiting to be unloaded from a slow moving wharf or bond store. The spirits, while some are a bit rough around the edges, are fine with mixers and much cheaper.

> **INFOTIP:** If you intend drinking alcohol other than beer, particularly outside establishments accustomed to tourists, play it safe by obtaining the permit from Indian Missions or Government of India Tourist Offices abroad. In India, permits can be obtained at these offices in Bombay, Delhi, Calcutta or Madras or at the tourist counters at Bombay International Sahar Airport or at the Taj Nahal Hotel.

You can buy Indian wines in good hotels by the glass or bottle. It is still fairly expensive in a flashy place but less than imported.

> **INFOTIP:** If you forget or run out of your duty-free and don't want to pay the high prices for mini- bar nips in your room, get a taxi driver to take you to an Indian liquor store. You may be asked to produce a permit. The prices for Indian-produced products are very reasonable, not so imports.

In Goa, where there is no prohibition, try the local hooch feni, made from either cashews or coconuts. It's strong straight. The two flavours are fairly distinctive, even when mixed - which they should be with soft drink or fruit juice. If you like either, buy a bottle. You will be unlikely to find it in most other parts of India.

Practical Information

Indian/International Restaurants

North Indian or 'Indian'

Copper Chimney, Rampart Row, Fort Bombay, behind the Prince of Wales Museum, Tel: 2041661. Renovation needed but top Tandoori, medium budget. Weekend reservations.

Daavat, Hill Rd., Baandra. Tel: 6402625. Modest decor. Spicy, rich, Moghlai and Hyderabadi.

Earthern Oven, Welcomegroup SeaRock Sheraton, Land's End, Bandra. Tel: 6425454, ex. 244. Intimate and expensive. Tandoori. No cutlery unless requested.

Gulzar, Hotel President, 90 Cuffe Parade,. Tel: 4950808 ex. 2553. Elegant, arched grandeur. Frontier food, Live Indian music 8 p.m. Baby marinated lamb leg, slow-fired north west style. Medium priced. Reservations 12 hours in advance.

Kandahar, The Oberoi, Nariman Point. Tel: 2025757 ex. 6111. Northwest Frontier cuisine. Refined atmosphere, antiques, sea and tandoor oven views. Meat eater's paradise, also vegetarian. Subtle spicing. Moistest murgh tikka in town. Reasonably priced. Cutlery on request. Reservations weekend and dinner.

Mela, Dr Annie Besant Rd., Worli, Tel: 4945656. Unique atmosphere of waterwheel, mirrors, posters and stream. All Indian cuisine, a trifle dear, with kebabs a feature. Reservations.

The Moghul Room, Oberoi Towers Hotel, Tel: 2025757, ex. 311. Moghlai food in a wonderful arched atmosphere. Evening music and Indian dance entertainment and an excellent buffet lunch. A large, comprehensive menu for meat lovers and vegetarians.

Delhi Durbar, 197 P. Bapurao Rd., Grant Rd., Tel: 357977. Moghlai. Air conditioned section. Ethnic vitality, particularly the tandoori. Also at Holland House, Colaba Causeway, Tel: 2025997.

Maharashtrian

Rambe Arogya Bhuvan, N.C. Kelkar Rd., Dadar. Small, unprepossessing decor but very good value and quality vegetarian with wonderful roti and chutneys.

Sindhi

Geeta Bhavan, Navjivan Society Building, Lamington Rd., Tel: 378079. Sindhi and Punjabi. Vegetarian. Busy, not luxurious, but cheap. Good dhal fry and Aloo Palak, (potatoes in spiced spinach.)

Practical Information

Gujarati

Chetana, 34, K. Dubash Rd., Rampart Row, Kala Ghoda opposite Jehangir Art Gallery, Tel: 244968. Gujarati and Rajasthani vegetarian with fixed lunch thali menu and a la carte dinner. Rajasthani decor. Excellent selection. Bookshop at rear.

Thali, Tara Baug Estate, Charni Rd., Tel: 355934. Closed Tuesdays. Gujarti Thali. A simple decor. Excellent charcoal-fired food which locals claim to be the best Gujarati in town.

New Aram Kutchi Restaurant, Mori Rd., Mahim Bus Depot, opposite Saint Michael's Church, Tel: 455510. Kutchi (a minority group) vegetarian. Nice decor. Wide variety of fragrant, spicy vegetables and many rotis. Reservations.

Parsi

Bombay A-1, 7 Proctor Rd., Grant Rd. Junction, Tel: 381146. Closed national holidays. Parsi, Chinese, Moghlai. Busy atmosphere. Speciality, stuffed pomfret wrapped in banana leaves as mentioned above. Reservations for groups.

The Landmark, RTI, 35 S. Patkar Rd., (Hughes Rd.,) Tel: 8226077. Closed Mondays. Parsi and Continental. Speciality, vegetarian Parsi wedding dish, Lagansara vegetable stew. Also kid gosht (marinated mutton with coconut milk and cashews.)

Piccolo, Horni Mody St., Tel: 274537. Closed Saturday p.m. and Sunday. Parsi. Clean, cool and homely. Specialty, the Parsi Sunday dish, mutton Dhansak.

Practical Information

Lotus Pond, Leela Panta Hotel

Bengali

Ashiana, Hotel New Bengal, Sitaran Building, B Block, D.N. Rd., Crawford Market, Tel: 331951-6. Bengali, Punjabi, Moghlai, Chinese. The only Bombay eatery offering Bengali food, essentially fish with groundnut oil or mustard.

Practical Information

South Indian

Kamat, Electric House, Colaba, Tel: 2874734. South Indian vegetarian. Snacks a feature plus thali. Very cheap.

Woodlands, Mittal Chambers, Nariman Point, near Oberoi Towers Hotel, Tel: 2023499. Closed Sundays. South Indian vegetarian. Plain decor. Excellent Idli steamed in banana leaves and inexpensive thali. Reservations for lunch.

Goan

City Kitchen, 301 Shahid Bhagat Singh Rd., (Frere Rd.) Fort, Tel: 260002. Closed Sundays and public holidays. Goan. Austere but cheap with good service. Typical Goan vindaloos. Stuffed roast piglet once weekly in December and January.

St. Mary Hotel, 120 St. Mary Rd., Mazgaon, Tel: 868475. Goan. Upstairs, tiny but cheap and worth the taxi ride from downtown. Good chutney fish fry and sliced beef tongue.

New Martin Hotel, 21 Glamour House, Strand Rd., Colaba. Goan and Mangalorean. Simple but providing opportunity to join eaters native to Goa and Mangalore. Super seafood and pork Sorpotel. Queueing may be necessary.

Chinese

The Great Wall, Hotel Leela Penta Kempinski, 1 km from Bombay International Airport, Tel: 6363669. Hunan cuisine (sweet, spicy, sour) is served in an environment of magnificent Chinese antiques in this opulent hotel, one of the few of 5 star rating in the city's suburbs. Expensive seafood. Reservations.

Chopsticks, 90A Veer Rariman Rd., Churchgate, Tel: 2049284. Hunan, Cantonese, Shanghaiese, Szechwan. Spicy, hot, sweet, sour and delicate reflections of each Chinese province. Reasonably priced. Reservations. Also another Chopsticks is at 354 Lingking Rd., Khar (West), Tel: 537789.

China Garden, Om Chambers, 123 August Kranti Rd., Kemp's Corner, Tel: 8280841. Chinese, Japanese, Korean, Vietnamese, Thai dishes. Cool, marbled, glittering. Famous clientele. Expensive, sumptuous and plentiful variety. Reservations essential.

Golden Dragon, Taj Mahal Hotel, Apollo Bunder, Colaba, opposite Gateway Of India, Tel: 2023366. Szechwan with some Cantonese. Excellent decor, atmosphere and service. Reasonable prices. Reservations.

Practical Information

French

Cafe Royal, Oberoi Towers Hotel, Nariman Point, Tel: 2025757. Closed Sundays. Classic French. Elegant, intimate atmosphere. Evening entertainment. Medium to expensive prices. Special, cheaper menus for airline crews. Superb cuisine and service. Reservations for dinner.

Rooftop Rendezvous, The Taj Mahal Hotel, Apollo Bunder, Colaba, Tel: 2023366. Split level, plush and lovely night views. Expensive, romantic, nightly dancing. Classic French specialties. Reservations.

The Society, Ambassador Hotel, Churchgate, Tel: 291131. Adventurous French menu for the unhurried. Reasonably priced. The Ambassador also has some French, Continental and Indian in its revolving restaurant, The Top. Reservations.

La Rotisserie, The Oberoi Hotel, Nariman Point, Tel: 2025757. French. Also, a few delightful Indian adaptions. Understated elegance. Reasonable to expensive prices, depending on your choices. Excellent value businessman's lunch. For French food connoisseurs. Reservations.

Italian

The Lido Bar Restaurant, Ritz Hotel, 5 Jamshedji Tata Rd, Churchgate. Tel: 220141. Italian (nearly,) Indian, Continental. Al dente pasta, pizza and saltimbocca authentically presented.   Trattoria, Hotel President, Cuffe Parade, Colaba/ Tel: 4950808. Warm, ambient atmosphere. Evening entertainment. Sunday lunch buffet. Excellent variety but specify al dente for your pasta. Reservations.

Muslim

Bade Mian Sheekh Kabab Stall, Tulloch Rd, Colaba, outdoors on the street behind the Taj Mahal Hotel. Street eating, rock bottom prices but delectable, hearty, meaty fare, essentially charcoal-grilled and worth the experience.

Al Maaida, 144, I.M. Merchant Rd., 8510257. Tel: 8510257. Clean, cheap, spit-roasted marinated meats and poultry in a small but inspirational menu.

Practical Information

Polynesian

The Outrigger, Oberoi Towers Hotel, Nariman Point, Tel: 2025757. Polynesian, Chinese and Indian. Very South Sea island atmosphere. More Chinese than Polynesian, but none-the-less tasty fare with a tropical tang. Exotic cocktails. Evening entertainment. Reservations dinner.

Salad Specialties

Saladero, Golden Gate Restaurant, Madame Cama Rd., Colaba, Tel: 2027989. Various salads served in addition to Moghlai and Chinese food.
See also La Rotisserie (French), Hotel Oberoi, Nariman Point. Very good lunchtime salad bar.

Seafood

Lobster Pot, SeaRock Hotel, Land's End, Bandra. Tel: 6425421. Surprisingly the only speciality seafood restaurant in Bombay. Lovely, quiet location. Lobster, pomfret, prawns and salmon. Evening entertainment. Prices according to your tastes. Reservations.

Thai

The Thai Room, Hotel President, 90 Cuffe Parade, Tel: 495808. Traditional Thai dishes, both spicy and mild. Reservations.

Coffee Shops

Most city hotels have coffee shops. Following are those which are open 24 hours.
Cafe Au Lait, President Hotel, Cuffe Parade, Tel: 4951090.
Oceanic, SeaRock Hotel, Land's End, Bandra, Tel: 535421.
Samarkand, Oberoi Towers Hotel, Nariman Point, Tel: 2024343.
La Brasserie, Hotel Oberoi, Nariman Point, Tel: 2025757.
Shamiana, Hotel Taj Mahal, Apollo Bunder, Tel: 2023366.
Coffee Shop, Centaur Hotel, Santa Cruz Airport, Tel: 6126660.
The Waterfall Cafe, Leela Penta Hotel, Bombay International Airport, Tel: 6363669.
Coffee Shop, Holiday Inn, Juhu Beach, Tel: 571435.

Practical Information

American (Fast Food Stalls/Establishments)
The following serve milkshakes, coffee, hamburgers, soups, pizza and icecream, etc:
Open House, Linking Rd., Bandra, Tel: 546118.
Open House, Veer Nariman Rd., opposite Churchgate Station, Tel: 221218.
Pizza King, 6 Tirupati Shopping Arcade, Warden Rd, Tel: 4926058.
Pizza King, Nyloc House, 254/D2, Dr. Annie Besant Rd., Worli, Tel: 4939757.

The following two establishments serve American-style sizzlers:
Kobe Sizzlers, Hughes Rd., near Sukh Sagar, Tel: 356652.
Sundance Cafe, Eros Building, Churchgate, Tel: 221286. (also serves Mexican, Continental, Chinese and sometimes French dishes.)

Lover's Leap at Dona Paula

Practical Information

Night Life

In addition to the theatre and cultural programmes often with dinner scheduled at intermittant times by hotels, (for example the Taj Mahal Hotel will organize one for a group) there are a few discos starting from between 9.30 p.m. and 10.30 p.m. and finishing at between 3 a.m. and 4 a.m. or whenever the guests want to leave!

The first opening at 9.30 p.m. is the Taj Mahal Inter-Continental's Nineteen Hundreds, which is the town's most exclusive night club. Middle-aged crowd. Interesting music.

Take Off, Airport Plaza, 70C Nehru Rd, Santa Cruz Airport, Vile Park (E,) Tel: 6123390. Frantic action, in a 60s mode for the energetic.

The Cellar, Oberoi Towers Hotel, Nariman Point, Tel: 2024343. Open 10 p.m. Crowded on weekends. Outrageous clothing if you wish. Good service, decor and music.

Studio 29, Pavilion, 29 Marine Drive, Tel: 2020060. Open 10 p.m. Young crowd. New Wave rock, jazz and pop. Fast action. Small dance floor.

The Cavern, Hotel SeaRock, Land's End, Bandra, Tel: 6425454/535421. Open 10.30 p.m. DJ. Cavenous atmosphere. Sharp dressing.

Xanadu, Hotel Horizon, 37 Juhu Beach, Tel: 6148000. Opens 10 p.m. More casual fun for seaside stayers.

Goa: Restaurants and Night Life

As Goa is very much a tourist resort, cultural programmes vary according to the season, so inquire of the Government Tourist Offices when and where these are likely to be, particularly in conjunction with dinner at a hotel.

Five Star Deluxe, five star and three star hotels listed under accommodation all have at least one restaurant. The Citade de Goa at Dona Paula has an excellent Portugese restaurant designed to achieve the atmosphere of a small town in Portugal. Live music. Several restaurants offer choice of buffet or a la carte at night. Night beach barbecues are popular at resorts in the non-monsoon season. The catch can be the guest's own.

Two beach restaurants of note open in the non-monsoon season are The Haystack, Arpora and Martin's Beach Shack, Dona Paula Beach. Naturally, fish and seafood are special.

An excellent guide to selective eating in Bombay is Flavours by Proeschel and Merani.

Practical Information

Shopping

Bombay is the market place for the whole of India and the visitor can buy goods that are not necessarily manufactured in India but smuggled in. Not that you are to know this but from Victoria Terminus to Colaba's end in the streets of South Bombay you will find about four kilometres of hawkers' stalls selling regular and smuggled wares from French perfume to laptop computers. Along this section you will discover almost anything you want to buy, but you will probably have to bargain for it. There are not too many fixed price stalls although some shops in the area have fixed prices.

Obviously the Colaba Causeway shopping street which starts from just behind the Taj Mahal Hotel, is not posh but there are good bargains and best goods to look for are leather (shoes and bags, particularly), silks, carpets and wooden goods.

The major markets have been discussed as you have walked through Bombay. Another good pavement shopping street, particularly for clothing, is Dr. D.N. Rd.

Other areas in addition to Crawford Market, Chor Bazaar and Zaberi Bazaar with its 3000 shops and stalls are Shahid Bhagat Singh Rd., Pherozeshah Mehta Rd., Mangaldas Market, M. Karve Rd. (where GITO is situated), and Linking Rd., Bandra.

For a kalaidescope of all Indian goods at fixed prices, check the wares on sale at Central Cottage Industries Emporium, 34 Chatrapati Shivaji Maharaj Rd., Tel: 2022491, just to see what Bombay and India has to offer.

This is just down from the Gateway Of India and very close to the Taj Mahal Hotel. Here you will find brassware, plated silver, sandalwood pictures and figures, ivory-inlaid wooden boxes miniature paintings on ivory, Kashmiri papier mache boxes, articles of mother-of-pearl and silver with enamelled work. From Agra and Jaipur are semi-precious stones inlaid into marble boxes and trays. There are soapstone carvings, wooden ducks, brass and copper inlaid into wooden articles, lamps (of particular interest are those hung with brass chains interspersed with elephants,) and village mud wall paintings. There are Gujarati figures carved from wood, also Hindu wooden dishes and wall hangings containing fine mirror work.

Do you need a silver-plated chair? From Rajasthan come Bichwai paintings on cloth, cushion covers and block prints on fabric in such items as bedspreads.

Also available are hand-loomed cotton furnishing fabrics, patchwork with mirror and embroidery details and Ikat weaves from Orissa.

Practical Information

There are kitchen and tea sets and cotton napery also leatherware of all sorts.

To carpets (also from Kashmir,) floor coverings, rugs and wall hangings, add silver ware in traditional designs and precious stones from all over India, particularly Jaipur and including aquamarine, topaz, onyx, turquoise, garnet, amethyst and filigree jewellery.

Clothing includes silk brocade scarves, wool shawls with Gandhiri (wool embroidered with mirrors,) wool with gold threads in purses, bags and pouches, silk and cotton saris, some of which are gold or silver threaded, caftans and clothes of all kinds that include mirror work. There are also designer clothes, some of which are created using traditional motifs but which are ultra modern in concept.

There are some magnificent items of furniture from Kashmiri walnut desks to dining settings inlaid with mother of pearl. Room screens are distinctive.

International doll collectors will find a wide selection of dolls of different sizes in the costumes of many States at very modest prices.

Practical Information

Other Government Emporia

Goods from several States are available at the World Trade Centre, Cuffe Parade. These include:
Chinar Jammu & Kashmir Government Showroon. Tel: 214365.
Gangotri, Uttar Pradesh, Government Emporium. Tel: 215497.
Himachal Pradesh Handicrafts Emporium.
Mrignayanee, Madhya Pradesh Handicraft Board. Tel 219191 ex.285.
Phulkari, Punjab Government Emporium. Tel: 215084.
Trimurti, Maharashtra Small Scale Industries Development Corporation. Tel 216056.

Other government shops are: Bihar Government Cottage Industries Sales Emporium, Dhun-Nur, P. Mehta Rd. Tel: 258328.
Black Partridge, Haryana Government Emporium, Air India Building, Nariman Point. Tel: 2024142 ex. 295.
Gurjari, Gujarat Government Handicrafts Emporium, Khetan Bhavan, J. Tata Rd. Tel: 221334.
Kairali Handicrafts Emporium of Kerala, Nirmal Building, Nariman Point. Tel: 2026817.
Khadi & Village Industries Emporium, 286 D.N. Rd. Tel: 263288.
Poompuhar. Tamil Nadu Handicrafts Centre, UN Pursaram, D.N. Rd. Tel: 292473.
Rajasthan Government Emporium, 230 D.N. Rd. Tel: 267162.
Shilpi Kendra, Majestic Hotel, Shahid Bhagat Singh Rd. Tel: 2028640.

Musical Instruments

Indian musical instruments are very popular purchases with foreign visitors. Government approved stores selling themn are:- R.S. Mayeka, 386, Sardar V Patel Rd. Haribhau Vishwanath, 419, Sardar V Patel Rd. DS Ram Singh & Sons, Bharati Sadan, Sardar V Patel Rd.

The GITO keeps detailed lists of shops it recommends in Bombay and several other tourist centres.

> **INFOTIP:** Check with GITO on the reliability of the stores offering to ship items to your home address.

Bombay shops are open between 10 a.m. and 7 p.m. Major hotels have shops but expect to pay more. Bazaars are open from 10 a.m. till 9 p.m. Credit cards and travellers' cheques are accepted at government emporia and the bigger shops but pay cash in the bazaars.

Practical Information

Rural Life

Shopping in Goa

Goa's markets are exciting, often offering the unexpected, including pottery and copper articles. Some of the handicrafts have distinctive Portugese influences. Government Emporia are:- Goa Handicrafts Rural & Small Scale Industries Development Corporation Ltd., has shops at Tourist Hostels in Panaji, Vasco da Gama and Mapusa and also at the Interstate Terminus in Panaji. Kashmir Government Arts Emporium, Hotel Fidalgo, Swami Vivekananda Rd, Panaji.
Kairali Arts & Crafts of Kerala, Hotel Fidalgo.
Mrignayanee, Madhya Pradesh Handicrafts Emporium, 4, Interstate Bus Terminus, Panaji.

Also the big resort hotels have clothing (some including some fascinating boutiques) and book shops.

Practical Information

Bombay, Gateway to India

Antiquities

Antiquities and objets d'art more than 100 years old are banned from being taken out of India. It is also prohibited that any skins of animals, including snakes, and the products made from them, used or unused, are included in accompanied or unaccompanied baggage.

To discover if purchases are antiquities or not contact the Director Antiquities, Archaeological Survey of India, Janpath, New Delhi -110 001, Superintendent Archaeologist, Antiquities, Archaeological Survey of India, Sion Fort, Bombay, Superintending Archaeologist, Eastern Circle, Archaeological Survey of India, Narayani Building, Brabourne Road, Calcutta - 700 013; Superintending Archaeologist, Southern Circle, Archaeological Survey of India, Fort St. George, Madras - 600 001 or Superintending Archaeologist, Frontier Circle, Archaeological Survey of India, Minto Bridge, Srinagar, Kashmir.

Sports and Athletics

BADMINTON   Cricket Club of India, Brabourne Stadium, Dinshaw Wacha Rd., Tel: 235313.

BILLIARDS AND SNOOKER   Cricket Club of India, Brabourne Stadium, Dinshaw Wacha Rd., Tel: 235313.

BRIDGE   Islam Gymkhana, Netaji Subhash Rd., Tel: 313292.

Practical Information

CRICKET   Bombay Cricket Association, Wankhede Stadium, Churchgate, Tel: 251562.
Cricket Club of India, D. Vacha Rd., Tel: 220262-284.

CYCLING   National Sports Club, Lajpatrai Marg, Tel: 4922817.

FISHING   Maharashtra State Angling Association, M.A. Kanchwalla & Sons, 97-99 Dhanaji St., Tel: 324395, 362992 (Temporary membership available. Day trips to Powai Lake arranged.)

FOOTBALL   Western India Football Association, Cooperage, Colaba, Tel: 2024020.

GOLF   Bombay Presidency Golf Club, Chembur, Tel: 5513670.

HOCKEY   Bombay Hockey Association, Charni Rd., Tel: 291271.

HORSE RACING   Contact GITO, Tel: 293144, for dates and times of meetings. Or, Royal Western India Turf Club, Khadya Marg, Mahalaxmi, Tel: 891122.

RUGBY   Bombay Gymkhana, Mahatma Gandhi Rd., Tel: 260311.

SQUASH   Cricket Club of India, Brabourne Stadium, Dinshaw Wacha Rd., Tel: 235313. Also Hotel Leela Penta has courts.

SWIMMING   M.G.M.O. Swimming Pool, Shivaji Park, Tel: 452062, 451014. Breach Candy Swimming Pool, Bhulabhai Desai Rd., Tel: 8224381, 364318. (Temporary membership available.) YMCA Swimming Pool, Bombay Central.

Also all five star deluxe and five star hotels have swimming pools and most health club facilities including sauna.

TABLE TENNIS   Khar Gymkhana, 13th Rd., Khar, Tel: 547129.

TENNIS   Maharashtra State Lawn Tennis Association, Cooperage, Colaba, Tel: 2023872.
Also Hotel Leela Penta has two tennis courts.

WRESTLING   National Sports Club, Lajpatrai Marg, Tel: 4922817.

YOGA   Kaivalyadhama, ICY Health Centre, N. Subhash Rd., Tel: 310494.

Practical Information

Sports In Goa

Goa State Council of Sports, Indoor Stadium Complex, Campal, Panaji.

BRIDGE Goa Bridge Association, Club Tennis de Gaspar Dias, Miramar, Panaji, Tel: 3862.

FISHING Most resort hotels organize trips. See GITO for other excursions.

HIKING AND TREKKING The Hiking Association of Goa, Care of Captain A. Rebello (president), Captain of Ports Office, Government of Goa, Panaji, Tel: 5070. (Organizes frequent hikes within Goa and trekking programme in December and January.)

SWIMMING Goa is drenched with beautiful beaches and all resort hotels have swimming pools.

> **INFOTIP:** Some of the private hotel beaches have safe swimming distances marked out. Do not deviate in case of hidden undertow.

Water Sports

Watersports, including windsurfing, yachting, boating, sometimes fishing, occasionally water skiing, para-sailing are organized by the following hotels. Check accommodation section for telephone numbers. Citade de Goa, Fort Aguada Beach Resort, Majorda Beach Resort, Oberoi Bogmalo Beach, The Taj Holiday Village, Aguada Hermitage, Hotel Chàlston, The Old Anchor, Hotel Silver Sands.

WIND SURFING Aqua Sport (India), 2nd floor, Ghanekar Building, Jose Falcao Rd., Panaji, Tel: 4706. (Facilities for wind surfing, para sailing, etc.)

YACHTING Yachting Association, P.O. Box 33, Panaji, Tel: 3261.

Telephone and Telegraph

Neither Bombay nor Goa have a system of public telephone booths operated by the government to the same extent of most western countries. However, many small businesses connected by telephone offer the use of

Practical Information

this phone to the visiting public for a fee usually double that of a local call from a public booth which is currently 50 paise. Internally, long distance telephone calls can be very frustrating to the tourist. The government is progressively updating the system but be prepared for long delays when booking a call and a connection that can sound as if you are speaking to someone on the moon.

International calls are also subject to long delays - it can be hours - although most five-star deluxe, five star and four star hotels have direct dialling facilities from guest rooms. You can place a collect call from India to the following countries: Australia, Belgium, Canada, France, Israel, Japan, Kuwait, Maldives, New Zealand, Norway, South Korea, Sweden, Switzerland, United Kingdom, USA, Spain, Thailand and West Germany. Expect to pay a service charge for the placing of a collect call.

The area code for Bombay is 022 which need not be dialled if you are calling within the district. Important service numbers are Inquiries and Complaints: 199. Long distance operator assisted calls: 183. Directory assistance: 197.

For direct dialling internationally, these are the international codes from India for the following countries:

Australia - 0061.
Austria - 0043.
Canada - 001.
Denmark - 0045.
West Germany - 0049.
Finland - 00358.
France - 0033.
Greece - 0030.
Israel - 00972.
Italy - 0039.
Japan - 0081.
Malaysia - 0060.
Netherlands - 0031.
New Zealand - 0064.
Norway - 0047.
Phillipines - 0063
Singapore - 0065.
Spain 0034
Sweden - 0046.
Switzerland - 0041.
United Kingdom - 0044.
USA - 001.

Five-star deluxe and five-star hotels in Bombay and Goa offer telex services and a few have facsimile transmission services for guests.

Practical Information

Time

Indian Standard Time (IST) is five and a half hours ahead of Grennwich Mean Time (GMT) and Central European Time.

Tipping

Tipping is expected (10 per cent) at restaurants and hotels where service charges are not included in the bill. More so than perhaps in any other country of Asia, tipping is expected from young boys who will fight themselves and you to lump your bags at an airport to a train conductor who will miraculously discover an empty seat on a train that has been booked out for weeks ahead. The tip given to the man who watches your shoes at temples and mosques is his livelihood. Tips are expected everywhere by anyone who performs a service. It at your discretion whether you tip taxi drivers.

> **INFOTIP:** Keep plenty of small denomination rupee notes. Also, if you photograph people, be prepared to be approached for a tip or suffer abuse. In Goa, this is less likely to happen.

Tourist Services

Government of India Tourist Office, 123, M. Karve Rd., (opposite Churchgate Station.) Tel: 293 144. Open 8.30 a.m. to 5.30 p.m. Monday to Friday and from 8.30 a.m. to 12.30 p.m. on alternate Saturdays and public holidays. Closed Sunday.

There are Government of India Tourist counters at Bombay Airport: New International Passenger Terminal, Sahar. Tel: 6325331, 6320700 ex. 253. Open 24 hours.
Bombay Airport Santacruz (domestic.) Tel: 6149200, 6122057 ex. 278-279. Open 24 hours.
GITO Counter, Taj Mahal Hotel, Apollo Bunder. Tel: 2023366. Open 8.30 a.m. to 3.30 p.m. Monday to Friday. 8.30 a.m. to 12.30 p.m. on alternate Saturdays and public holidays. Closed Sunday.

Indian Tourist Development Corporation (ITDC), Nirmal Building, 11th floor, Nariman Point, Tel: 2023343, 2026679.

Practical Information

State Government Tourist Offices

Maharashtra Tourism Development Corporation, CDO Hutments, Madame Cama Rd. Tel: 2026713, 2027762. Also at Express Towers, 9th Floor, Nariman Point. Tel: 2024482, 2024584.

Government of Goa Tourist Counter, Bombay Central Station. Tel: 396288. (Closed Sundays and public holidays.)

In Goa: Directorate of Tourism, Tourist Home, Pato Bridge, Panaji. Tel: 5583, 5715, 4757.

Government of India Tourist Office, Communidada Building, Church Square, Panaji. Tel: 3412.

Tourist Information Counter, Interstate Bus Terminus, Panaji. Tel: 5620.

Tourist Information Counter, Dabolim Airport. Tel: 2644.

Tourist Information Centre, Tourist Hostel, Margao. Tel: 22513.

Tourist Information Centre, Tourist Hostel, Vasco da Gama.Tel: 2673.

Outside India, the Government of India Tourist Office maintains offices in many countries and can provide the prospective visitor with up to date information.

Australia: 65, Elizabeth St.,Sydney, NSW. Tel: (02) 232 1600, 232 1796.

Austria: 1-E-11 Opernring, 1010, Vienna. Tel: 587 1462.

Canada: 60 Bloor St, West Suite, 1003, Toronto, Ontario. Tel: Tel: (416) 962 3787, 962 3788.

Practical Information

Flower Seller in North India

France: 8 Boulevard de la Madeleine, 75009, Paris.
Tel: 42658386.
Federal Republic of Germany: 77-111 Kaisserstrausse, 6000, Frankfurt. Tel: 235 423, 235 424.
Italy: Via-Albricci 9, Milan, 20122, Tel: 804 952, 805 3506.
Japan: Pearl Building, 9-18, 7-Chome Ginza, Chauo-ku, Tokyo 104. Tel: (03) 571 5062, 63.
Kuwait: P.O. Box 4769, Sadoun Al-Jassim Building, Fahad Al-Salem St., Safat 13048. Tel: 242 6099, 242 6088.
Malaysia: Lot No 203, 2nd Floor, Wisma MPI, Jalan Raja Chaulan 50200, Kuala Lumpur. Tel: 425 285, 425 301.
Singapore: 5th Floor, Podium Block, Ming Court Hotel, Tanglin Rd. Tel: 235 5737.
Sweden: Sveavagen 9-11, 1st Floor, S-III 57, Stockholm.Tel: (08) 215 081, 101187.
Switzerland: 1-3 Rue de Chantepoulet 1201, Geneva.
Tel: (022) 321 813.
Thailand: Singapore Airlines Building, 3rd Floor, 62-5 Thaniya Rd., Bangkok. Tel: 235 2585.
United Arab Emirates: Tourist Promotion Office, Post Box 12856 DNATA, Dubai. Tel: 695 398.
United Kingdom: 7 Cork St., London WIX 2 AB.
Tel: (01) 437 3677- 8.
USA: 3550 Wilshire Boulevard, Room 204, Los Angeles, California, 90010. Tel: (213) 380 8855.
Also: 230 North Michigan Ave., Chicago, Illinois, 60601. Tel: (312) 236 6899, 236 7869, 236 7270.
Also: 30 Rockefeller Plaza, Room 15, North Mezzanine, New York, NY 10020. Tel: (212) 586 4901-3.

Practical Information

Tours

Half Day, Bombay City

1. Gateway Of India, Jain Temple. Hanging Gardens, Kamla Nehru Park, Mani Bhavan, Aquarium, Prince of Wales Museum. Departs 9 a.m. and 1.45 p.m. daily, except Monday. Reservations: ITDC, GITO and Travel Corporation of India (TCI,) Mon Repos, off Arthur Bunder Rd., Colaba, Tel: 245225.
2. Places as above plus Jehangir Art Gallery and Council Hall. Departs 9 a.m., daily except Monday.
3. Alternatively places as in tour 1 plus Worli Dairy, Nehru Science Centre and Jehangir Art Gallery. Departs 2 p.m., daily except Monday. (Reservations for tours 2 and 3, MTDC, or MTDC Counter at GITO).

Full Day Tour Bombay Suburbs

1. Vihar Lake, Observation Point, Kanheri Caves, National Park, Lion Safari Park (closed Mondays) and Juhu Beach. Departs 10 a.m. daily. Reservations, MTDC.
2. Half or full day Elephanta Tour (subject to weather during monsoon.) Launches depart every hour from 9 a.m. to 2.15 p.m., returning after every four hours. Inquiries, Tel: 2026364.

One Day, One Night Tour

Nasik, on the banks of the Godavri River, a place of pilgrimage, and Shirdi, related to the mystic saint Sai Baba. Departs 8 p.m. and returns to Bombay 9 p.m. Daily departures. Reservations MTDC.

Two Day (Three Night) Tour

Aurangabad - Ajanta - Ellora. Departs 8.30 p.m. returning to Bombay 7.30 a.m. on the 4th day. Reservations, MTDC. Also departing 7.15 p.m. and returning to Bombay at 7 a.m. on the 4th day. Reservations, ITDC.

Three Day Tour

Fly Bombay-Goa early p.m., return p.m. day 3. Reservations Indian Airlines or GITO.

Practical Information

Tour Operators and Agencies

The following firms have been approved by the Department of Tourism, Government of India:

ABC Travel Consultants, Jehangir Villa, N. Parekh Marg. Tel: 215373, 215371.

Aero Agency, 112 Meadow St. Tel: 274425-99.

Ambassador Travels, 14, Embassy Centre, Nariman Point. Tel: 234714, 234748.

American Express International Travel Division, Majithia Chamber, D.N. Rd. Tel: 2049421, 2048291.

Asiatic Travel Service, 12 Murzban Rd. Tel: 2048151, 2044168.

Atlantic Pacific Travel Service, Alankar Building, Dr. A.B. Rd. Worli. Tel: 4930551, 4932746.

Balmer Lawrie, 5 J.N. Heredia Marg, Ballard Estate. Tel: 268106.

Bathijia Travels, New Silk Bazaar, 491 Kalbadevi Rd. Tel: 311207-8.

Blue Skies, 28 K. Dubash Marg. Tel: 242771.

Cox & Kings, Grindlays Bank Building, D.N. Rd. Tel: 2048724, 2043065.

Diners World Travel, 213 Nariman Point. Tel: 224949.

Eastman Travel & Tours, 21 Dalamal Chambers, New Marine Lines. Tel: 293523, 290342.

Everett Travel Service, 1 Regent Chambers, Nariman Point. Tel: 245133.

Freight Carriers, 43 Tamarind Lane. Tel: 292371.

Govan Travels, Poonam Apartments, Dr. A.B. Rd. Tel: 4924760, 4924537.

Happy Travels, Century Bhavan, Dr. A.B. Rd. Tel: 4224028, 4224135.

Hermes Travels, Dhiraj Chambers, 9 Waudby. Tel: 260666.

Hind Musafir Agency, Khorshed Building, Sir P.M. Rd. Tel: 2861544.

Indwest Travels, Amardeep Mahal, Banda Pather Rd., Vile Parle. Tel: 6142561, 6143745.

Indtravels, Neville House, Ballard Estate. Tel: 265761-66.

Mackinnon Travel Service, 4 Shoorji Vallabhdas Marg. Tel: 268026, 267012.

Mercury Travels, Oberoi Towers Hotel Shopping Arcade, Nariman Point. Tel: 2025527, 275384.

Mercury Travels (Tour Department,) 27 World Trade Centre, Cuffe Parade.Tel: 214380, 219191 ex. 222.

Orient Express, 359 D.N. Rd. Tel: 2871047.

Patvolk Travel Services, 19 J.N. Heredia Marg, Ballard Estate. Tel: 261531, 266751.

Sita World Travels, 8 Atlanta, Nariman Point, Tel: 240666, 231954.

Practical Information

SOTC Travels & Tours, Vasvani Chambers, D. Vacha Rd. Tel: 243775, 222861.
Thomas Cook, Cooks Building, D.N. Rd. Tel: 2048556, 2046101.
Trade Wings, 30 K. Dubash Marg. Tel: 244334.
Trans Travels, 4 Jain Chambers, 557 S.V. Rd.
Bandra. Tel: 6425412-3.
Travel Corporation of India, Chandermukhi, Nariman Point. Tel: 2021881, 2027120.
Travel India Bureau, 7 Arcadia, Nariman Point. Tel: 231774, 231487.

Guide Service for Tourists

Approved tourist guides for local sightseeing in Bombay and Goa can be arranged through the GITOs and by ITDC or MTDC in Aurangabad (Ajanta and Ellora.) The fees, modest by most western standards, are based on half day and full day employment, coupled with the number of persons - 1-4, 5-15 and 16-40. The standard charges are for English-speaking guides. In Bombay, guides fluent in French, German, Italian, Spanish, Russian, Japanese and Arabic can be engaged, if available, for a small additional fee.

Herbs and Spices

Practical Information

THE METRIC SYSTEM

Length

1 millimetre	0.04 inches
1 centimetre	0.39 inches
1 metre	1.09 yards
1 kilometre	0.62 mile

Practical Information

Converting kilometres to miles is as simple as multiplying the number of kilometres by 0.62.(e.g. 10km's x 0.62 6.2 miles)

Converting miles to kilometres is done by multyplying the number of miles by 1.61 (e.g. 60mi x 1.61 96.6km's)

Capacity

1 litre   33.92 ounces
             1.06 quart
0.26 gallons

Converting litres to gallons, multiply the num'er of litres by .26. (e.g. 20l x .26 5.2 gallons)

Converting gallons to litres multiply number of gallons by 3.79. (e.g. 10 gal x 3.79 37.9l)

Weight

1 gram 0.04 ounces
1 kilogram 2.2 pounds

Converting kilograms to pounds, multiply number of kilos by 2.2. (e.g. 55 kg x 2.2 121 pounds)

Converting pounds to kilograms, multiply number of pounds by .45. (e.g. 100 pounds x .45 45 kilos)

Area

1 hectare 10000m/sqr or 2.47 acres

Converting hectares to acres, multiply the number of hectares by 2.47 (e.g. 10 ha x 2.47 24.7 acres)

Converting acres to hectares, multiply the number of acres by .41 (e.g. 40 acres x .41 16.4 ha)

Temperature

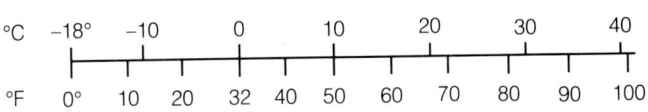

PART V
Business Guide

BUSINESS GUIDE

Contents

Banks
Business Briefing
Business Publications
Business Services
Business-Trade Organizations
Conference Facilities
Credit Cards
Currency Exchange
Import and Export of Currency
Messenger Services
Social Business Associations
Trade Fairs and Exhibitions
Translators

Business Briefing

Main Industries: Textiles, electronic goods, engineering, chemicals, pharmaceuticals, plastics, paper, leather, wood, crude oil, mining products (Goa.)
Main agricultural products: Rice, wheat, tea, coconut oil, palm oil, coffee, spices.
Main imports: Machinery, fuels and lubricants, iron and steel.
Main exports: Cotton goods, ready-made garments, polished diamonds, gems, jewellery, leather and leather goods, iron ore, tea, coffee, silk, carpet, arts and crafts, perfumes and incense.
Principal trading partners: USA, Japan, West Germany, U.K. Belgium, USSR, Saudi Arabia and France.

Exchange, Import/Export of Currency

There is no import or export of Indian currency allowed. However, this does not apply to rupee travellers' cheques. Foreign banks keep rupee balances with their Indian agents and the procedure is to draw on these balances to issue rupee travellers' cheques to visitors.

There are no restrictions on the amount of foreign currency or travellers' cheques brought into India but a Currency Declaration of amounts exceeding US $1000

Business Guide

carried at the time of arrival will ensure that unspent amounts can be converted back. Exchange of foreign currency other than through authorized banks and money changes is an offence. Visitors trading on the black market risk receiving counterfeit currency.

There is no limit on the import of travellers' letters of credit or travellers' cheques but the amount must not exceed on departure that declared to Customs on arrival. Receipts from banks or moneychangers should be held against departure and reconversion. Foreign currency drafts, irrespective of value, must be declared. The exception of US$1000 applies only to currency notes, bank notes and travellers' cheques.

Should a visitor wish to import specialized equipment or articles other than those listed at the beginning of the Practical Advice for tourists section, application must be made to the Chief Controller of Imports and Exports, Udyog Bhavan, New Delhi. The particulars of each article, the reason for import and the approximate value must be stated.

Foreign and Indian banks open from 10 a.m. to 2 p.m. Monday to Friday and from 10 a.m. to noon Saturdays. A few hotels have 24-hour banks. Travellers' cheques can also be cashed with the cashier in the bigger hotels.

A few banks have evening hours, closing on one week day. All banks are closed on national holidays and June 30 and December 31. Making outward payments through the Reserve Bank is frustrating. It is preferable to remit through a draft or mail transfer and keep all receipts.

Banks

Foreign Banks and Approved Money Changers in Bombay

American Express, D.N. Rd. Tel: 2048196.
Bank of America Express Towers, Nariman Point. Tel: 2023431.
Bank of Montreal, Maker Tower-E, Cuffe Parade. Tel: 213584.
Bank of Oman Ltd., Air India Building, Nariman Point. Tel: 2046290, 2873305.
Bank of Tokyo, Jeevan Prakesh, P.M. Rd. Tel: 2860564.
Banque National de Paris, 62 Homji St. Tel: 253487.
Barclays Bank Int. Ltd., Maker Tower-F, Cuffe Parade. Tel: 212797.
British Bank of Middle East, 16 Veer Naiman Rd. Tel: 296077, 2048203.

Chartered Bank, 25, M. Gandhi Rd. 2047198.
Citibank NA, 239 D.N. Rd. Tel: 258853.
Grindlays Bank, M Gandhi Rd. Tel: 270162.
Hong Kong and Shanghai Banking Corporation, 52 M.G. Rd. Tel: 275319.
Nova Scotia Bank, Mittal Tower B, Nariman Point. Tel: 232822.

Indian Banks

ABN Bank, 19 Veer Nariman Rd. Tel: 252331.
Andhra Bank, 18 Homi Modi St, Fort. Tel: 2046160.
Bank of India, Express Towers, Nariman Point. Tel: 2023020.
Pheroze Framrose, Air India Building, Nariman Point. Tel: 2022790.
State Bank of India, Bombay Samachar Marg (at Centaur Airport Hotel until 10 p.m.) Tel: 2863896.
Union Bank of India, Union Bank Building, 239 Backbay Reclamation, Nariman Point. Tel: 2024033.
Reserve Bank of India, Foreign Exchange Department, New Central Office Building, Bhagat Singh Rd. Tel: 295602.

Credit Cards

American Express, Majithia Chambers, 276 Dr. Dadabhai Naoroji Rd. Tel: 2048291.
Diners Club, Raheka Chambers, 213, Nariman Point. Tel: 244949.
VISA, ANZ Grindlays Bank Ltd., 90 Mahatma Gandhi Rd. Tel: 270007.
Mastercard, Care of agent at Bank of America, Express Towers.
Telex: 112152. (For cash advances.) In the event of losing Mastercard, call collect from anywhere in the world 1-314 275 6690.

Business-Trade Organizations

Bombay Chamber of Commerce and Industry, Mackinnon Mackenzie Building, 4 Shoorji Vallabhdas Marg, Ballard Estate. Tel: 264681.
Maharashtra Chamber of Commerce, Oricon House, 6th Floor, 12 K. Dubash Marg, Fort. Tel: 244548.
Directorate of Industries, Government of Maharashtra, New Administrative Building, Madam Cama Rd. Tel: 2028616.

Office of the Controller of Import and Export Trade, New Central Government Offices Building, New Marine Lines.
Maharashtra Industrial Development Corporation, Marol Industries Area, Mahakali Rd. Tel: 6325451.
State Industrial and Investment Corporation of Maharashtra, Nirmal Building, Nariman Point.
Directorate of Export Promotions, CGO Building, New Marine Lines. Tel: 298299.
Bombay Stock Exchange, Phiroze Jeejeebhoy Towers, 25th Floor, Dalal St. Tel: 275626.

Goa

Chamber of Commerce and Industry, Goa Chamber Building, Rua de Ormuz, Panaji. Tel: 4223. 3420.
Economic Development Corporation, EDC House, Atmaram Borker Rd., Panaji. Tel: 4541-4.
Goa, Daman & Diu Industrial Development Corporation, Saraswati Mandir Building, 18th June Rd., Panaji.
Tel: 6201-5.
Goa Small Handicrafts Development Corporation, Next to Don Bosco High School. Gov. Pestana Rd., Panaji.
Tel: 5702.
Industrial Finance Corporation of India Ltd., EDC House, 5th Floor, Atmaram Borker Rd., Panaji.

Business-Social Organizations

Bombay Rotary: There are 21 Rotary Clubs in Bombay District. Bombay Central meets Fridays at 1.15 p.m. at the Oberoi Towers Hotel. Inquire there for contacts throughout Bombay. Bombay Club meets at the Taj Mahal Hotel Tuesdays at 1.15 p.m. Inquiries, tel: 253806.

Bombay Lions meet at the West End Hotel on alternate Friday evenings. Tel: 219141.

Radio Club, 147 Arthur Bunder Rd. Tel: 245025.

Diners Club Executive Centre, Raheja Chambers, Nariman Point. Tel: 245383.

Bharatiya Vidya Bhavan, Chowpatty. Tel: 8118261 (for information on philosophy or religions.)

Foreigners Regional Registration Office, near Mahatma Phule Market. Tel: 4150446.
For informal, social meetings with Bombay families in their homes, call GITO on 293144.

Business Guide

Goa

Lions and Rotary Clubs are care of Hotel Mandovi, Panaji. Tel: 6270.

Business Publications

Newspapers: The Times of India, The Hindustan Times, The Hindu, The Indian Express, The Telegraph and The Statesman. Also USA Today.
Magazines: Mainstream, Sunday and India Today. Also The Economic Times, POB 213, Bombay. Tel: 4150271. Financial Express, Express Towers, Nariman Point. Tel: 2022627. Journal of Industry and Trade, Ministry of Commerce, Delhi.

Business Services

World Trade Centre off Cuffe Parade.
Business Centres with secretarial, telex, FAX, telephone and meeting room facilities are localed at the following hotels, (see accommodation guide for addresses and telephone numbers.) The Oberoi, (24 hours,) The Oberoi Towers (24 hours,) The Leela Penta Kempinski, The Taj Mahal Hotel, Hotel President and.Hotel SeaRock.
Hotel Airport Plaza, Hotel Nataraj, Hotel Sands, Hotel Ritz (secretarial service and telex.)
Hotel Centaur: Telex and photocopier.
Hotel Horizon: Telex.

Goa

Citade de Goa (telex and secretarial service.)
The Aguada Hermitage (telex.)
Fort Aguada Beach Resort (telex.)
Hotel Oberoi Bogmalo (secretarial services.)
Taj Holiday Village (telex.)
Hotel Fidalgo (secretarial service.)
Hotel Ramada Beach Fatrade (FAX and telex.)

Messenger Service

Skypack. Check the nearest courier to you with your hotel telephone operator.

Business Guide

Trade Fairs

Bombay is location for many trade fairs but as these vary from time to time, contact your GITO at home for current updates.

Translators and Interpreters

These are available through GITO, Bombay. Tel: 293144-5.

Conference Facilities

Both Bombay and Goa are well equipped for large and small conferences from 10 to 1500 delegates in meeting rooms in from two to five star deluxe hotels. See accommodation for capacities and numbers of conference rooms.

Air India is a member of the International Congress and Convention Association (ICCA) and its Congresses and Exhibitions Section, with 45 offices in India and 150 in foreign cities, will direct conference organizers to the venue most appropriate, make all arrangements and assist in the planning of any pre and-or post conference tours. There is a wide range of discounts on individual and group airfares for conferences. These may also be appropriate on Indian Airlines internally as IA is also an ICCA member, along with several international standard-hotels.

Major Airlines with offices in Bombay

Many of these offices are situated on Nariman Point and are open during regular business hours of 10 a.m. to 1 p.m.; 2 p.m. to 5 p.m. Monday to Friday; 10 a.m. to noon Saturday. A few take round-the-clock reservations. Phone to check. Buses for the airport leave the Air India building, opposite the Hotel Oberoi Towers, the city's tallest building, at Nariman Point. Times are every hour from 4 a.m. to 7 a.m, 9 a.m. to 10 p.m. and midnight to 2 a.m.

Air India, Air India Building, Nariman Point, 2024142. An office is also in the Taj Mahal Hotel, Apollo Bunder.

Aeroflot, Nirmal Building, Ground Floor, Nariman Point, 221743.

Business Guide

Air Canada, Hotel Oberoi Towers, Nariman Point, 2027512, 2027632.

Air France, Maker Chambers, 6, Nariman Point, 2025021.

Air Mauritius, Hotel Oberoi Towers, Room 7-8, Mezzanine level, Nariman Point, 2024723 ex 646, 2028474.

Alitalia, Industrial Assurance Building, Veer Nariman Road, Churchgate.222144, 222112.

Alyemda Democratic Yemen Airlines, Hotel Oberoi Towers, HC level, Nariman Point,2024343.

Bangladesh Biman, Airlines Hotel Building, 199 J. Tata Rd.221339,220676, 223342,224580.

British Airways, Vulcan Insurance Building, Veer Nariman Point, 220888.

Cathay Pacific, Taj Mahal Hotel, Apollo Bunder, 2029112-3,2025580, 2023366.

Czechoslovak Airlines, 308/309 Raheja Chambers, 213 Nariman Point, 220736, 220766.

Egypt Air, OPriental House, 7,J Tata Rd, Churchgate Reclamation,221415.

Ethiopian Airways, Taj Mahal Hotel, Apollo Bunder, 2024525,2029378, 2028787.

Garuda-Indonesian Airways, 5 Raheja Centre, Nariman Point, 243075, 243725.

Gulf Air, Makar Chambers, 5 Nariman Point, 2021441, 2021626, 2021777, 2021667.

Iberia, Ambassador Hotel, Veer Nariman Rd, 2041131.

Indian Airlines, Air India Building, Nariman Point, 2023031.

Iran National Airlines Corporation, Sunder Mahal, N. Subhash Rd., 297037, 297025, 253524, 297070.

Iraqi Airways, Mayfair Building, Veer Nariman Rd, 221399, 221217.

Business Guide

Japan Airlines, Raheja Centre, Nariman Point, 244245.

Kenya Airways, 199, J. Tata Rd, near Astoria Hotel, Churchgate.220015.

KLM, opposite Ritz Hotel, J. Tata Rd, 2214013, 221185, 232625.

Kuwait Airways Corporation, 86 Veer Nariman Rd, Churchgate, 298351 and on Saturdays only 312395.

Lufthansa, Express Towers, Nariman Point,2023430, 2020887.

Malaysian Airlines, STIC Travel & Tours, Maker Arcade, Cuffe Parade, 211431.

Middle Eastern Airlines Co., J. Tata Rd., Churchgate, 224580.

Pakistan International Airlines, Hotel Oberoi Towers, Nariman Point, 2021373, 2021598, 2021480, 2021456.

Pan American Airways, Taj Mahal Hotel Apollo Bunder, 2029020, 2023366.

Phillipine Airlines, Airlines Hotel Building, 199, J. Tata Rd, 224580.

Polish Airways (LOT) Maker Arcade. Room 6, Cuffe Parade, 211440.

Qantas Airways, Hotel Oberoi Towers, Nariman Point, 2029297, 2026373, 2029288, 2020343.

Sabena (Belgian World) Airlines, Nirmal Building, Nariman Point,2023240, 2023284, 2023817, 2022724.

Saudi Arabian Airlines, Express Towers, Nariman Point, 2020519, 2020199, 2020181.

Scandinavian Airlines, World Trade Centre, Cuffe Parade, 219191, 215207.

Singapore Airlines, Air India Building, Nariman Point, 2023365, 2023316.

Swissair, Maker Chambers VI, 220 Nariman Point, 222402, 222539.

Syrian Arab, 7 Stadium House, Veer Nariman Rd, 226043, 226143, 220460.

Thai International, World Trade Centre, Cuffe Parade, 219191, 215207.

Yemenia, Ambassador Hotel, Veer Nariman Rd, 244068, 243059.

Zambian Airways, Maker Chambers, 11 Nariman Point, 241251, 222944, 243666.

Alphabetical Index

A
Adil Shah Palace 84
Advance Planning 119
Afgan Church 61
Ahura Mazda 21
Airlines, Major 190
Ajanta Caves 96
Akbar the Great 23
Alcoholic Drinks 156
Architecture 40
Art Galleries 125-127
Art Gallery, Jehangir 54
Ashoka 20, 31

B
Babysitting 127
Back Bay 63
Banks 186
Barbur 24
Barmer Jaisalmer 13
Battery Island 50
Bazaar, Bhendi 74
Bazaar, Chor 74
Bazaar, Zaveri 73
Beaches of Bombay 78
Beaches of South Goa 92, 94
Belim 95
Bhagwan Mahavir Sanctuary 91
Bibi-ka-Maqbara 96
Black Jews 21
Bogmalo Beach 83
Bose Subhash Chandra 37
Brahma 18
Buddha 19
Buddhism 19
Business Briefing 185
Business Organisations 187
Business Publications 189
Business Services 189

C
Candepar River 91
Chatrapati Shivaji 49
Chatrapati Shiravji 93
Children's Entertainment 127
Chola Kingdom 32
Chowpatty Beach 64
Christianity 22
Churches, South Goa 88
Cinemas 128
Climate 11
Clothing 119
Coconut Day 64
Commerce 16
Consulates 142
Corbett National Park 13
Crime 146
Culture 30
Currency 123, 185
Customs 122

D
Dance 129
Daulatabad Ford 97
Death 145
Delhi Sultanate 33
Dilras Banu Begum 96
Documents 119
Dr Garcia da Orta 47
Dravidians 24
Dudhsangar Waterfall 91
Duty Free Imports 123

E
Education 16
Electricity 125
Elephanta Caves 50
Elephanta Island 49
Ellora Caves 96, 98
Entertainment 125
Entry Regulations 122
Exhibitions 129

F
Fardapur 98
Fatemi Mosque 74
Festivals 130-133
Films, Fabulous 75
Flora Fountain 56
Flora and Fauna 12
Fort Aguada 94
Fort Bassein 78
Fort Bombay 48

G
Gandhi Indira 38
Gandhi Mahatma 37
Gandhi Rajiv 38
Ganesh Chaturthi 64
Gateway of India 47

Index

Gautama 19
Geology and Geography 11
Getting Around Bombay 135
Getting Around Outside
        Bombay 137
Getting to India 124
Goa 79
Golden Goa 82
Government 14
Guide Service 179
Gujurati 65
Gupta Dynasty 32
Guru Nanak 20

H
Haji Ali's Mosque Tomb 70
Hanging Gardens 67
Help 142
Hinduism 18
Hindus 31
History 30
Horniman Circle 57
Hotels 105

I
Indian Languages 28
Indus Valley 30, 41
Industry 16
Interpreters 190
Islam 24

J
Jahangir 42
Jain Temple 66
Jainism 20
Jehangir Nicholson Museum 60
Jnana Yoga 19
Jogeshwari Caves 78
Judaism 21

K
Kabir 20
Kamala Nehru Park 65
Kanha National Park 14
Kanheri Caves 76
Karma 19
Karma Yoga 19
Khajuraho 42
Koli 61
Krishnagiri Upvan 76

L
Lake Nalsaroval 14
Lake Powai 76
Lake Tulsi 76
Lake Vihar 76
Lakshmi 18
Libraries with Books
        in English 148
Lion Safari Park 76
Lok Sabha 15
Lost Property 146

M
Maem 93
Mahabalipuram 41
Mahalaxmi Racecourse 70
Mahalaxmi Temple 70
Malabar Hill 63
Malabar Hill 65
Mandovi River 82
Mandovi River 93
Maps 100, 195
Mapusa 93
Maratha 61
Maritime Museum 50
Markets 73
Maurya Dynasty 31
Medical Emergencies 144
Medical Tips 120
Meeting People 25
Memorial Musueum,
    Mani Bhavan 69
Messenger Service 189
Metric System 180
Mongol-Dravidians 25
Motoring 147
Mount Kailash 98
Mughal Empire 33
Mumbadevi 47
Municipal Corportation 58
Municipal Gardens 84
Museums 125-127
Music 134

N
Nadir Shar 34
Nariman Point 60
Nataraja 51
National Centre of Perf Arts 60
Nehru Jawaharlal 37
Nehru Pandit 38
Nehru Planetarium 71
Niceties of the North 93
Nightlife 151-165

O
Odds and Ends 120
Old Goa 88

Index

P
Parsi Towers of Silence 68
Parsis 21
Parsvanath 66
Peoples of India, The 24
Police Emergencies 145
Ponda 90
Prince of Wales Museum 53
Publications in English 148
Punjab 20

Q
Quest for Discovery 9
Qutb-ud-din-Aibak 42

R
Radaut Tahera 74
Radio 134
Raj 35
Raj Bhavan Temple 66
Rajabai Clock Tower 54
Rajya Sabha 15
Ramganga River 13
Religions 18
Religious Services 150
Rental Vehicles 147
Replacement
    Certain Items 146
Restaurants 151-158
Royal Asiatic Soc. Library 57

S
Safa Masjid 90
Saraswati 18
Scytho-Dravidians 25
Se Cathedral 88
Seminars 133
Shahjahanabad 42
Shakti 18
Shiva 18
Shopping 166
Shri Maguesh 90
Siddhartha 19
Sikhism 20
Sirrdl School of Art 73
Social Organisations 188
South Goa 88
Sports 170-172
State of Maharashtra 47
State of Pakistan 38
State of Rajasthan 13
State of karnataka 41
Sultan Bahadur Shah 47

T
Taj Mahal 42
Tamil Nadu 42
Taraporewala Aquarium 63
Telephone and Telegraph 172
Television 134
Temples and Traffic 63
Temples of South Goa 88
Theatre 134
Time 174
Timur 33
Tipping 174
Tirthankara 66
Tour Operators 178
Tourist Services 174
Tours 177
Trade Fairs 190
Trade Organisations 187

U
Uihas River 78
Univerisity, Bombay 54

V
Vajreshwari Hot Springs 78
Vanguinim beach 81
Vardhamana Mahavira 20
Vasco da Gama 83
Vedas 31
Victoria Albert Museum 72
Victoria Gardens and Zoo 72
Victoria Gardens 51
Victoria Railway Terminus 57
Vishnu 18

W
What to Bring 119
World Trade Centre 63
Worli Dairy 72

Y
Yogisvara 51

Z
Zarathusthra 21
Zoroastrianism 20

Notes